A Celebration of Food
from the
Four Seasons of the World

by

The Mount School

The Mount School - A Celebration of Food from the Four Seasons of the World

Preface

Food occupies a central position in any family and community, and the Mount School is no exception. No public occasion passes by without the provision of food, from canapés in the dining room after prize-giving to the Japanese food stall at the Winter Bazaar. No school fundraising appeal can match the revenue generation of a Bake Sale or sweet stall at break time. Food gives structure to our days. School meals remain a perennial concern of the Mount School Parliament, and if there's one thing that can be relied upon to galvanise the whole school into action, to divide opinion and initiate debate, it is food.

The Mount School is a multicultural community and we are proud to have representatives of almost every ethnicity and religion in the world. Every pupil brings their own tastes and traditions with them and, as the title reflects, this anthology is an opportunity to celebrate that diversity.

In the preface to the second Mount School Cook Book published in 1996, the Head Teacher at the time reflected on the many changes the school had seen since the publication of the first edition and predicted, accurately, that the third edition of a cook book would not appear until the 21st Century. Little did she imagine that it would take the form of an e-book! Our school has continued to grow and develop, as I hope the variety of recipes in this anthology demonstrates.

The recipes in this collection have been chosen for a variety of reasons. Some are served on special occasions, to celebrate or mark religious occasions. Others are everyday dishes, served to nourish family members and strengthen family bonds. All of them, though, have been chosen because they are greatly loved, as shown by the accompanying stories, poems and art. I hope that you will try preparing many of them for your families and friends, and enjoy discovering for yourselves the pleasure they have given to others.

This entire anthology has been edited by pupils in Year 9 and all the recipes that appear here have been contributed by school pupils, their parents and staff.

I hope you will join me in thanking the enthusiasm of the staff and the girls for creating such a sumptuous literary feast.

Catherine Cozens

Headteacher
The Mount School
www.mountschool.com

The Mount School is a long established GSA Independent day school for girls, located in Mill Hill village, North London. Girls join our nursery from three years old and leave as confident and responsible young adults at the age of 16. We are proud of our excellent exam results, small class sizes, dedicated teaching staff and the real sense of community that can be felt throughout the school.

Cover artwork by Clare Pitt.

ISBN 978-1-909227064
mardibooks ©2012
www.mardibooks.com

From the Editorial Team

Welcome. We are the Mount Mardi team: Amber Codron; Lauren Perkins; Mariam Haddad; Nour Borghol and Sophie Shaban, all aged 14 -15, who before this experience knew nothing about publishing. We chose to be involved because we wanted to achieve something on our own, demonstrating self-reliance and independent learning. On top of this we have learnt various practical and life skills such as people skills, working as a team and becoming far more I.T literate.

There have been many pros and cons during this process such as organisation and time management, but we have learnt a lot and even through the struggles we were able to meet the deadlines we set and are still smiling and talking to each other.

In fact, we thoroughly enjoyed what has been an amazing experience and an incredible achievement.

We would all love to be a part of Mount Mardi team in the future and be able to grow and continue to widen our knowledge of the editing and publishing world.

Whilst the anthology is primarily a recipe book, we wanted to incorporate something more than this. As a TV dinner society it is our generation that is missing out on the sharing and communal aspects of traditional meals. What we have tried to convey through this collection is a taste of food from around the world from multi- cultural communities and world geographies. To beautify our creative oeuvres and further titillate your taste buds we have incorporated art work from across the junior and senior years at The Mount School.

Year 4 and 6 have been working very hard and enthusiastically making food related images using a variety of media including paper collage, paint and pencil. Years 7 to 10 have also used multi-media to create prints and other images to adorn the writing across the four seasons. Their work on borders has enabled the words to be lifted off the page.

We hope you enjoy our mouthwatering creation.

Autumn

My Peasant Poem

Being a Peasant, is highly unpleasant
We have to wake up at the crack of dawn
To feed the animal and get some corn.

The food we eat is terribly rotten,
Stew and pottage I wish were forgotten,
As a replacement, I eat some lamb,
Or a joint of smokey ham.

The working hours we all do,
Buys us enough for a bit of stew.
The only decent thing to eat,
Is beer or cider and berries sweet.

One day we were starving hungry,
So we ate the dog, oh the little darling!
If you think that is the worst,
Listen to this final verse....

Sometimes we have nothing to eat,
This leads from starvation to one last beat
But this is such a normal thing
That nobody cries at the deceased.

Being a peasant is highly unpleasant. How would you feel?

Rachel Price – Yr.7

Medieval Food

Rules to what you could eat
The rich ate meat
The poor ate wheat

Berries, nuts and honey
The rich had too much money
Eating white bread
While the peasants lived in a shed

Cider, beer and wine
So smooth, so fine
Herrings, eels and fish
All made a delicious dish

The peasant's food was dark bread
While the nobles were well fed
Figs and oranges bought at the fair
The poor did not have enough to share

Poor were born and raised in a cottage
All they ate was bread and pottage
Too much chicken, too much geese
The rich were gluttons, they became obese

For the rich, salted meat served as stew
Before the poor could eat they had work to do
Spices such as cinnamon and ginger
The peasants had to eat off their fingers

A big manor house with several fireplaces
In through the door came 50 faces
Birds were roasted on a spit
Poor peasants didn't even get a bit

The key to food was farming
The rich thought they were handsome and charming
Peasants worked all day and night
But they only got a little bite

Leak pottage was very well known
Peasants so skinny you could see their bones
Pigs slaughtered throughout the year
Lords and villagers also ate deer

Breakfast: three meat dishes all were mainly fishes
Dinner: 4 to 6 courses with wine and ale
The numbers went up on the weighing scale
Supper: woodcock and pigeon pie, also served with ale and wine

Breakfast: Dark bread made of rye, with some ale
The bread was probably stale
Dinner: Ploughman's lunch which was dark bread and cheese also served with
a few peas
Supper: if lucky a bit of meat to go around this is what peasants ate in the town

Peasants grew barley and rye
No food meant they were going to die
Pottage was a stew made of oats
This is what kind of food went down their throats

Janvi Patel – Yr.7

Medieval Food

Once upon a time, there was a family. This family were not rich but their hearts were as pure as gold. They were peasants and worked for Lords and Chiefs but they didn't mind. In fact, they loved working. The only thing that was bothering them was money. They needed money to actually run their farm. But this was about to change. The family were famous for their original chicken soup but had to give the money they made to the Lords.

"Mother, Leslie won't come out of her coop or let me in!" Jimwood (the youngest sibling) shouted from the kitchen in their farm house.

"Well, ask Dad to move the coop and then maybe she'll come out!" said the mother (Margret) as she   came down the stairs. She was in a rush because the community women were having a meeting today and she was late!

"Dad's gone to Canterbury to sell some of the piglets!... Oh, fine, I'll try and move it myself!" Jimwood ran to the garden.   Margret had no time to protest. If she did, she would be just that little bit later than she already was and she didn't want that!

"Bye!" Margret ran out to the horse and cart waiting for her.

"Mother?!" Shouted Bridget (the eldest sibling) who awoke to find her mother and father gone. Before she could find Jimwood, there was a rather meek knock at the door. With slight hesitation, she opened the door to find Kind Richard II stood with two strong knights by his side. Her eyes widened and she curtsied down to him.

"Your Majesty, may I help you?" she struggled with her words.

"Yes, you see, one of my finest sources has told me that his sister bought the most 'delicious' chicken soup for you, I am here to taste some. I am actually very fond of chicken soup but have never tasted a good making of it." He pushed past her and looked around. "Where are your parents?"

"Oh, I am very sorry your Highness but they are both out!" She was still shocked.

"Oh dear! Well, do you have any spare chicken soups that you hopefully made earlier?" His voice sounded disappointed.

"Yes! Yes we do your majesty!" Bridget ran to the cupboard and pulled out a fresh chicken soup. It had just been put on the stove and was shoved in the cupboard to cool. "This was for our dinner tonight, but, we can always just eat some of our rye bread and dripping."

"Oh, well, I am very sorry......may I try it now?" The king asked for a spoon and tasted the soup. "How amazingly splendid!" Jimwood heard all of this from in the garden and came rushing in. He ground to a halt and also bowed down to Richard.

"Your Highness, May I ask what this commotion is about?" he stuttered.

"Yes! I have just tasted your family's chicken soup and I adore it. You and your family are invited   to my 15th Birthday buffet! I will send you the details on an invitation later this week."

"Why thank you, your Highness!" Both Bridget and Jimwood thanked Richard II as he left through the door.   After telling their parents the shocking, yet extraordinary news, both Margret and her husband Jack were over the moon. The invitation came earlier that week, leaving them enough time tell everybody. The invitation also stated that they had to bring at least 5 large bowls of chicken soup along with them. At the banquet, many high-class Lords commented on their soup that it became much liked and very well-known. The best part about this was that the money that they made from the chicken soup didn't have to go to the Lords, the King had insisted that they kept the extra money.

Now, whenever you eat chicken soup, hopefully, it will remind you of this miraculous story!

Shabri Sanghani – Yr.7

A Peasant's Lot

I think I am the poorest person in the world, but then everybody says that these days. Everybody has got so grumpy after the plague.

I wake up at 3am and feed my animals. I sometimes think that they get more food than me. I have no nice clothes at all; all I have is 1 rag. I always walk down the street and see rich people in their gorgeous robes eating lamb and rabbit. They are all such show offs. At 6am I have to go to Mr Green's house. I accidentally woke him up at 11am by cleaning. He was so mad he got the broom and hit my back so hard that I flew to the ground with a thud. It really hurt. I thought I was going to die. I could barely move.

At 2pm I finally ate lunch, once I had given Mr Green his rabbit, peas, potatoes and carrots. One day I tried to steal some of his food because I was really hungry. He got so mad, he didn't give me food for a week. I thought that I was going to die.

Once I had finally fed him, he moaned about how little food he had (I would give anything to have his food.) I got to have my food, which was the world tiniest bowl of stew (there was not even any meat in it!)

Whenever I tell a rich person my life story, hoping they would give me some money, they are selfish and gave me nothing but a dirty glance.

Amy Grossmith-Dwek – Yr.7

Medieval Food Poem

Eating with our fingers, rabbits, pigs and hens,
Poor eat animals after slaughtered,
Rich ate fish,
Whittle was used to slice chunks of meat,
Cooked and prepared in the manor kitchen,
Rich eat with tableware, with plates made of wood, pewter or silver,
Poor drink ale, rich drink wine,
They eat soups made from beans, peas, herbs and spices,
Ate and served,
Like they deserve.

Ellie Smith - Yr.7

The Peasant And The Lord

A long time ago, many years before now,
A certain dinner made one peasant frown.
This is the story of the peasant and the lord,
The peasant played on a pipe, which the lord adored.
It all started on a Sunday afternoon,
Where the town crier announced,
that Eppleton's feast will be soon.
All barons were allowed to attend,
And the Lords most loyal friends.
But could Peasants go to the feast?

Word came out, that if an invitation was sent
You could go to the Lords dinner.
The peasant waited for days for his invite.
What if the dinner was on that night?
Suddenly, there was a knock on the peasant's door,
He was not anxious anymore.
A short stubby man appeared and invited the peasant to the Lords dinner.
The day came, and the peasant walked
Into the Lord's Castle and was astounded.
On a huge table was a cooked piglet on a tray.
The peasant looked at it in a hungry way.
"Oh, this pig looks delicious" he said,
"This would taste great with a slice of rye bread"
He sat down and ate peacock with wine and rabbits in gravy.

"There is so much food I've never seen.
From places I'd probably never been.
I'm just a poor man, who only eats bread and pottage,
And lives in a beaten down, wooden cottage"
Lord Eppleton sat beside the peasant and said
"Peasant, why are you so sad?
After this feast you will be full of glee,
So enjoy yourself and stick with me"
The Lord and the peasant ate and had some rum,

Till, there was no space in their tum.
The peasant turned   to the lord and said
"This is the best and first feast I've ever been"
The Lord replied " There will be plenty more if you stick with me"

Antonia Williams - Yr.7

Foul Food

Rich and Poor,
The poor wanted more,
The rich ate fish pie,
But the poor were ready to die.

The poor ate dogs,
The rich ate frogs.

Berries and honey
For the peasants so yummy,
But the rich had too much money.

Pork, geese and sheep,
One pig the poor could keep,
Eating pottage,
In the peasants cottage,

Eating salted fish,
The poor could only wish,
While the rich ate whale,
The poor drank ale.

The rich had gear,
But the poor drank beer.

Grace Kindall - Yr.7

Arepas

Ingredients:

- 2 glasses of water
- 2 glasses of corn flour
- A sprinkle of salt

Apparatus:

- Bowl
- Spoon
- Frying pan
- Oven –pre heat at 250 degrees

Method:

1. Add the salt and corn flour to the bowl and mix with your hands or a wooden spoon
2. Pour the water into the mixture
3. Knead the dough together until there are no lumps
4. If it is too sticky – add more flour and vice versa if too dry.
5. Roll into a ball
6. Split the ball and roll in to smaller ones, pat, turn and lay out with width of 5.08cm and 2.54 cm in length
7. Heat oil in pan and when it starts to sizzle add the dough
8. Leave for 10 minutes and keep flipping until it is evenly brown
9. Add the Arepas but decrease heat to 200 degrees and leave for about 15 -20 minuets
10. When they feel hollow cut open sideways (like pitta bread pockets) or eat whole- but leave to cool.

Amelia Rawlinson - Yr.10

The Wedding

Once upon a time there lived a poor family who worked very hard on their farm looking after their crops and animals. The family were peasants whose diet consisted of pottage and rye bread. One day the peasant family were working hard in the field when a letter arrived, it was an invitation to Henry III's daughter's wedding. The family were so happy and excited that they stopped working and went off to make outfits for such an occasion. They were distracted for many weeks and the farm suffered as a consequence.

Finally, the wedding day arrived and the family walked down the hill to the castle in their finery. When they entered the big hall they saw the magnificent food placed on the trestle table. The food consisted of a boar's head, curdled and garlanded. The family were amazed to see so much food, there was even swan, pig, hens and a blackbird. There was also some amazing spices. They danced the night away and then the wedding came to an end. When they got home they looked around the farm and realised they had been so preoccupied with getting ready for the wedding, they had not been looking after the animals and crops properly, but the family had realised something that being poor was better than being rich because working hard is the best reward of all.

Shabri Sanghani - Yr. 7

Be-All, End-All Chicken Soup

For this story I'm going to explain the so called 'Jewish remedy' or as it's more commonly known chicken soup. In the Jewish religion for Shabbos every Friday night, we all sit down as a family and have a meal consisting of chicken, roast potatoes, vegetables and chicken soup. I have been doing this for as long as I can remember.

The real reason for the 'Be-All, End-All' part is all because of a contest that we decided to have in my family. My grandma made her version of chicken soup, my mum hers and my dad his (my granny did not make her version because well she can't cook).

This cooking contest was held only last year. And every one who participated had one week to prepare and make chicken soup with a twist. My dad put meatballs in his, my mum put chicken pieces in hers and my grandma did it the traditional way.

The following week my grandpa, Saskia (my sister) and I tasted the chicken soups, a bowl of each. First up was my grandma's soup. She presented it in a nice bowl and it tasted very nice and obviously my grandpa, being my grandma's husband, said it was divine, better than anything he had ever tasted!

Then came my mums soup it was presented very nicely in a square bowl with a warm little challah roll on the side it was even better than my grandma's all the chicken pieces where very nice too.

Then last of all came my dad's soup presented in a cup he claimed that all the bowls where used and put a little herb on top and Saskia, being as fussy as she is, refused to eat it because it had an herb and a big yucky meatball in it. This soup was quite nice but not the best of the lot.

Then Saskia, my grandpa and I had a decision of who's was the best. We all decided on my mum's and hers was crowned the 'Be-All, End-All 'chicken soup!

Recipe

Serves however many the pots can hold!

Ingredients:

- 4 medium parsnips – peeled
- 2 large onions – peeled and left whole
- 3 large leeks – trimmed
- 4 medium celery sticks- trimmed
- 1 to 2 turnips
- 6 carrots – peeled
- Whole chicken portioned – including neck
- Salt and pepper for seasoning
- Cold water
- Large stock pot

Recipe:

Place the chicken pieces in the large stock pot.
Fill with cold water.
Bring to the boil
Skim off any fat and dirty water that rises to the top (this is called shunning).
The dirt will be grey, white froth floating on the top. Once this has stopped appearing reduce the heat to a simmer and put in all the vegetables.
Simmer for at least 3 hours.
Turn off the heat and allow soup to cool.
When at room temperature, place the soup in the fridge and keep overnight.
Before the meal, take the soup out of the fridge and bring to the boil and then simmer.
Serve with challah roll.

Chicken soup always tastes better the next day.
Knaidlach - matzo balls or Kreplach taste delicious in the soup.

Natasha Livingstone – Yr.9

Chicken Soup - Jewish Penicillin

This is a firm family favourite for many reasons:
- First food for all children
- Passed from generation to generation
- Something we have every Friday evening
- Because it is delicious for the body and soul

Ingredients: For 15 - 20 portions

- 3-4 chicken carcasses
- 1 pack of chicken giblets (internal organs)
- 6 chicken wings
- 1 pack of chicken necks
- 1 large turkey neck
- 1 swede
- 8 carrots
- 1 celery
- 1 tomato
- Chicken/vegetable stock to taste

Method

Put all the meat in the largest possible pot you have - it will need to be very deep.   Peel the swede and add.   Peel and chop the carrots into large chunks, chop the celery into similar chunks.   Add all the ingredients to the pot. Cover with cold water and bring to the boil.   When boiling, a layer of dark foam will form, spoon off and discard.   Once finished producing foam - season with several tablespoons of stock, salt and pepper (optional).   Turn the heat down to medium and let simmer for 4/5 hours.

Once cool enough remove and discard the carcasses but keep the bits in a separate bowl.   *We keep it all, except the swede and carcasses.*   Strain the clear soup and store in fridge for about 24 hours.   In fridge the fat will rise to the top and solidify - spoon this off and heat the soup with the bits in it or on the side as you prefer.

For serving on a Friday evening the soup is put on early Thursday, turned off at lunchtime, strained early evening and put in fridge.   It is then taken out Friday early evening, skimmed and heated.

Serve with noodles and matzo balls (kneidle) and lots of love.

Hettie Virchis - Yr.4 and her family

Clam Chowder

This is a lovely simple recipe which can be made with a variation of ingredients depending on what you like.

Ingredients:

- 3 slices bacon, diced
- 1 cup chopped onion
- 3 cups diced potatoes
- 1 bottle (8 ounces) clam juice
- 1 teaspoon salt
- 1/4 teaspoon pepper
- 2 cans (approximately 7 ounces each) minced clams
- 3 tablespoons flour
- 2 cups half-and-half
- 1 cup milk

Preparation:

Cook bacon until crisp in a Dutch oven or large, heavy saucpan. Remove bacon to paper towels with slotted spoon; drain. Add onion to bacon drippings; sauté until softened. Add potatoes and clam juice, salt, and pepper. Cover and simmer for about 15 minutes, or until potatoes are tender. Remove from heat. Add minced clams with their liquid. Whisk flour into milk; add to chowder with half-and-half. Cook over medium heat, stirring constantly, until clam chowder thickens and bubbles, or about 3 minutes.Clam chowder recipe serves 4.

Riko Ota - Yr.2

Salmon Fried Rice

Ingredients (serves 4):

- 3 cups of rice
- 3 eggs
- 1 tablespoon of vegetable oil
- 1 garlic clove, finely chopped
- 1 large onion, finely chopped
- 200g smoked salmon, chopped
- 1 tablespoon of sesame oil
- 1 tablespoon salt
- ½ tablespoon pepper
- 1 tablespoon soy sauce
- 1 tablespoon sesame

Method:

1. Cook rice using rice cooker. Put into a bowl and cover with a paper towel
2. Refrigerate until cold
3. Add beaten eggs and mix together
4. Heat a wok over high head and add vegetable oil, swirl to coat.
5. Add garlic. Cook until smell
6. Add onion. Cook until translucent
7. Add salmon and stir-fry for 1 minute
8. Add rice and eggs and stir-fry until heated through
9. Add sesame oil, salt, pepper, soy sauce and sesame

Yukari Sado - Yr.5

Pizza Poem

Cheese and tomato
On a pizza base,
We need more topping
To solve this case!

Pineapple is my favourite
In its yellow skin
Just lay it on the pizza
Chopped nicely thin!

Pizza is definitely
My favourite treat
You can put almost anything on it,
Any way is delicious to eat!

Imogen Frost - Yr.6

Nonna's Lasagne

This recipe is my Grandma's recipe or Nonna as I call her. Unfortunately she cannot make it anymore. Even though the recipe has been taught to me and many other members of my family it never tastes as good as hers.

Every time I eat this dish I remember family gatherings, eating it under the hot sun in her garden with cold lemonade and the neighbour's chicken clucking next door. My cousins and I driving everyone else crazy by being noisy and laughing hysterically over the most absurd thing which no one else could understand. But there was one time that the lasagne tasted better than any other. We were staying in my Auntie Lily's house, which had a beautiful view over the lake; it looked especially pretty at night, with all the lights looking like little stars. It was chilly outside but toasty inside the house. We all sat at the table and Nonna brought out the lasagne and the whole pan was gone within half an hour. We talked and laughed- it was truly the best lasagne I had ever eaten. Afterwards we had fruit, cheese and then coffee and biscuits.

That was when Nonna could remember the recipe, that was when she could remember all of us. That's why I love lasagne, it brings back good memories and new ones can be made while making and eating it.

Recipe

In this recipe there are three main components, the meat sauce, the béchamel sauce and the pasta.

Ingredients for Meat Sauce:

- Minced Beef 500g
- 3 finely chopped carrots
- 1 large onion finely chopped
- 2 celery sticks finely chopped
- 1 tin of chopped tomatoes
- Half a tea spoon of tomato puree
- 2-3 sage leaves
- Salt

Method

Firstly, soften the onion, carrots and celery. Add in the minced meat and wait for this to brown. Add the tomatoes and tomato puree, season with salt. Let this cook over a medium heat from 30-45minutes.

Ingredients for Béchamel Sauce:

- 1 litre of milk
- 60 g of flour
- 60g of butter
- Salt
- (Additionally Parmesan cheese for topping)

Firstly, put the flour in a pan then mix in a little bit of milk to make a thick paste. On a medium heat, add in the rest of the milk, butter and a pinch of salt. Stir until you can no longer see the butter.

The last step of the recipe is to boil the lasagne sheet pasta.

Finally, the combining of all three components. First put a layer of pasta at the bottom of the pan, put some of the meat sauce and béchamel sauce, sprinkle parmesan cheese then put another layer of pasta, repeat this process until the oven dish is full. On the final layer of meat and béchamel sauce with parmesan do not put a layer of pasta on top.
Leave in the oven for half an hour at 180 degrees Celsius.
This dish feeds 4-5 people.

Description:

This dish is perfect for family gatherings as it is a great dish to share with other people. Lasagne is nice to have throughout the year but especially during autumn because of the colours; the reds, oranges, browns and yellows, just like the lasagne. It is also a warm hearty dish which fills you up easily.
This dish is the perfect combination of flavours and textures. The smooth pasta, the bitter yet sweet tomatoes, the sharp celery, the salty parmesan, with all these dancing around in your mouth.
It goes nicely with salad and garlic bread.

Mariam Haddad - Yr.9

Ella's Favorite Recipe - Pasta with Parma Ham

Ingredients:

- 6 shallots,
- 2 clove if garlic,
- 4 courgettes,
- 12 mushrooms
- 300 grams of Fusilli (pasta),
- 1 small tub of crème fraiche,
- 140 grams of Parma ham,
- 2 handfuls of parmesan,
- Some fresh basil to decorate.

Method:

1. Fry shallots with garlic, add courgettes and mushrooms until soft.
2. Add crème fraiche and parmesan cheese, put this to one side.
3. Cook pasta in another saucepan for ten minutes.
4. Add Parma ham at the last minute to mushroom sauce.
5. Drain the pasta, stir in mushroom sauce to pasta and then sprinkle with fresh basil leaves and serve.

Ella Brown - Yr.5

Lamb Irish Stew Recipe

Ingredients:

- 1 tablespoon olive oil
- 2 pounds boneless lamb shoulder, cut into cubes
- Salt and pepper to season
- 2 large onions, sliced
- 4 carrots, peeled and cut into large chunks
- 1 small chopped suede
- 1 pint of stock
- 4 large potatoes, peeled and cut in half
- 1 tablespoon chopped rosemary
- 1 large leak chopped
- 2 tablespoons of pearl barley
- 1 bay leaf
- Worcester sauce

Method:

Heat oil over medium heat in a large stockpot. Add lamb pieces and cook, stirring gently, until the lamb is browned. Season with salt and pepper.

Add the onion, carrots, suede, and leak and cook gently with the meat for a few minutes. Stir in the stock and add the bay leaf, a splash of Worcester sauce, and the pearl barley. Cover and bring to a boil before turning the heat down to low. Simmer for 1-2 hours.

When the meat is tender, stir in the potatoes, and simmer for 20minutes, before adding rosemary. Continue to simmer uncovered, until potatoes are tender but still whole. Serve piping hot in bowls.

Ellen McDermot - Yr.11

Irish Stew

Our Family Stew:

- 700g stewing steak
- 1.5 litres beef stock
- 5 large peeled potatoes
- 4 large carrots, chopped
- 2 large onions chopped in quarters
- 3 tablespoons of cornflower
- 3 teaspoons of pepper
- 2 tablespoons of sunflower oil
- 2 bay leaves
- A generous pinch of salt
- A good handful of parsley

Method:

1. Preheat the oven 200 Celsius
2. Place the stewing steak, cornflower and pepper in a resealable bag. Seal the bag and give it a good shake so that all the steak pieces have a coating of flour and pepper.
3. Heat a tablespoon of sunflower oil in a large frying pan and brown half the steak pieces. Transfer the steak pieces to a casserole dish. Repeat with the rest of the meat.
4. Fry the onions in the meat juices in a large frying pan for 2 minutes, (add another drop of oil if necessary.) Transfer the onions to the casserole dish.
5. Add the carrots, beef stock, sea salt and bay leaves to the casserole dish and stir through. Add the potato slices on top, season with black pepper and cover with a lid.
6. Transfer the casserole dish to the oven and cook for 1 ½ hours.
7. Serve straight from the casserole dish to some large bowls and sprinkle the parsley on top.
8. Serve with wholemeal bread and enjoy!

Sophie Shaban – Yr.9

Potato and Spinach

Ingredients:

- Potatoes – half a kilo cut in small cubes
- Spinach- 1 kilo washed
- Onions-2 medium finely chopped
- Tomatoes- 2 medium chopped
- Salt-to taste
- Turmeric-2 pinch
- Red chilli powder-to taste
- Oil-6 tablespoons

Method:

1. Heat oil in the pan, and add the onions.
2. Sauté onions for 2-3 minutes then add the potatoes, salt, chilli, turmeric and tomatoes.
3. Simmer on medium heat for 5 minutes and then add the spinach.
4. Mix together and leave on medium heat for 20-25 minutes.
5. Keep mixing after every 7-8 minutes.
6. Serve hot with naan bread.
7. Enjoy

Afzaa Altaf - Yr.5

Dolma Recipe

Ingredients:

- 1 lb ground lamb (Beef may be substituted, or you can also mix lamb and beef together)
- ¼ lb white rice (you may also use basmati or bulgur wheat – but do not use brown rice for this recipe).
- 2 medium onions, chopped very finely
- 1 small can of tomato paste
- ¼ cup of parsley, chopped finely

You will also need:

- Assorted small vegetables for stuffing for example green and yellow squashes, small eggplants, yellow, red and/green sweet peppers.
- Some lemon juice for the steaming process (about ¼ cup).
- Some cabbage, grape or other sturdy green leaves to line the pot with – to be discarded after cooking.

Directions:

- Mix the Dolma stuffing mixture and let it marinate, covered, in the refrigerator for several hours – overnight is best.
- With a table spoon and a sharp peeling knife, carefully cut and scoop out the insides of the vegetables to form nice cavities for the stuffing – set aside these insides (except the peppers) for a healthy, light soup.
- Fill each dolma about 2/3 full with the stuffing mixture.
- Take a covered pot and line it well with the cabbage or other greens.
- Pour about 3 cups of water and the lemon juice into the bottom.

- Place each dolma into the pot, standing upright to form a single layer on top of the greens. The dolmas may be lightly touching, but do not crowd them together, as when the rice cooks, they will expand a bit.

- As one layer fills, place a loose layer of greens on top and add another layer – and so on, until you have used all the vegetables. Put the strongest vegetables – such as the onions or the eggplants on the bottom and the most tender (tomatoes) on the top.
- Cover the top layer with another layer of greens, cover the pot and place on top of the stove over a low to medium heat. If the water is absorbed, gently add more.
- Steam lightly until the rice and meat has been cooked and the vegetables are tender.
- Take off the heat and let the entire pot sit covered for at least a half hour before uncovered.

Sarah Mansour - Yr.9

Recipe For Peppers Stuffed With Rice

Products: (serves 6)

- 6 medium bell peppers
- 1 medium onion
- 200 g basmati rice
- 2 vegetable stock cubes
- ½ tin tomatoes
- 1 tbs salt
- 2 tbs oil
- 1 tbs paprika
- 1 tbs basil, oregano and mint
- ½ pot plain Greek style yogurt

Preparation:

Remove the stalks of the peppers. Add a pinch of salt in each pepper. Shallow fry the finely chopped onion in the oil for about 2 – 3 min or until golden brown. Add the rice and shallow fry for another 2 min, stirring constantly. Make the stock with the vegetable stock cubes and 1 ½ litres hot water. Add to the rice and stir well. Stir until the rice is ready. Add the tomatoes and stir again. Add the salt, paprika and the herbs, you can also add herbs by your choice. Stuff each pepper with the mixture, place them in a baking tray and add 1 litre water. Bake in the oven on 200 C or gas mark 5 for about 1 – 1 ½ hrs. Turn each pepper so it is evenly cooked. If you have some mixture left over, you could still serve it as it makes a delicious meal. Serve hot with a 2 tbs of plain yogurt.

This recipe is a variation of peppers stuffed with minced meat and rice. If you like your meat, all you have to do is mix the minced meat (about 250 g) with the rice (about 150g) well and make sure the meat is throughly cooked before you stuff the peppers with the mixture.

Annie Lalova - Staff

Jallof Legends

The story of Jollof rice happened in the origins of Wolof and their people. The king of Wolof had a very beautiful and fertile wife called Jollof and since they had quite a lot of children she made this recipe for them which they loved. She boiled rice and once it was ready she fried the onions poured tomato sauce and many spices she mixed them together and served.

As it was so lovely her husband asked her to cook it for his guests during one of their festivals and the people loved it and named it after her in her honour.

Spicy Sensation

I look to my left through my glassy brown eyes,
My mother comes to me with her big warm smile.
She has a bowl in one hand and tissue in the other.
She knew I was upset and she did the thing most mothers would do
Cheer their child up.

I grab the bowl with appreciation towards my mother
I look at the food in the bowl. The orange and red fiery delight
I knew once I have one bite of the rice my troubles would have been chewed away.
The sweet, tangy, spicy aroma weaved its way up my nose.

Mouth watered at the ready I take a bite the spices sting my taste buds sending me to cloud nine.
The fluffy rice is the cloud that sends me back to earth as I have to swallow.
As it wanders down the narrow passage it warms it up.

I breathe out like a dragon breathing fire
The spices aren't gone they are tenderly hugging my mouth
The next bite is better than the first.
Bang! Crack! Pop! There is a party and fireworks are definitely the main event.

Bite after bite my troubles fade away
I look at the bowl. Empty. I smile knowing my mother did the best thing ever.
She gave me jollof rice.
The thing that can change anyone's mood.

Anne-Marie Durojaiye – Yr.10

Menu!

🎶 Chicken Pottage.
Thickened sauce with a paste of cooked ???
Can be served with meatballs.
Rated ★★★★★

🎶 Whitebait patina
Mouth-watering whitebait omelette
served to your standards!
Rated ★★★★★

🎶 Duck with turnip
Succulent duck, cooked to absolute
perfection! Your choice of turnip.
Rated ★★★★★

Apricot and Coffee Cake

My Apricot and Coffee Cake Haiku Poems

My flavoursome cake,
Is very soft and spongy,
It tastes so divine!

My nutritious cake,
Looks very mouth-watering,
It's so sweet to eat!

My heavenly cake,
Tastes so crunchy and fruitful,
It's so delicious!

Recipe

The recipe that I have chosen is called Apricot and Coffee Cake. I especially like this cake because it contains apricot and nuts which give it a pleasant taste.

This cake is probably best known to be eaten in autumn because of the cakes colours; Most of the ingredients that are included in this cake are usually popular in autumn.

This cake is from Turkey, a country in the middle of Europe and Asia.

I am fond of this cake because it tastes very nice and delectable.

Ingredients

- 8 dried apricots
- 3 eggs at room temperature
- 1 cup of powdered sugar
- 1 cup of cooking oil
- 1 tea cup of milk
- 3 tablespoons of powdered coffee
- 1 tablespoon of baking powder
- 2 tablespoons of nut pieces
- 250 grams (may need more flour.)

Utensils

- 1 bowl
- Mixer
- Strainer
- Knife
- Baking Tray

Method

1. Break the eggs into a bowl.
2. Add in the sugar and mix with a mixer.
3. Mix for 5 minutes until the sugar dissolves.
4. Add in the cooking oil, milk and the coffee and mix until smooth.
5. Take a strainer, and add the flour and the baking powder into the mixture.
4. Cut the apricots into quarters and add it to the mixture.
5. Pour the mixture into an oiled baking tray and dust it with nut pieces.
6. Heat the oven to 170 degrees and cook for 30-40 minutes.
7. When cooked, immediately serve.

Eda Yukselen - Yr.7

Banana Cake

Ingredients:

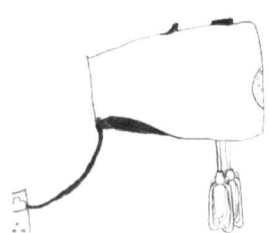

- 4oz of softened butter or margarine
- 6oz of sugar- caster sugar
- 8oz o self-raising flour
- 2 eggs
- 2 large or 3 medium ripe bananas

Method:

- Set the oven to gas mark 4; 180C to heat up the oven.
- Grease the tin you are going to use.
- Mash up the bananas
- Cream the sugar and butter and then add the eggs.
- Mix the bananas together and the other mixture consisting of sugar, butter and eggs.
- Add the flour in the final mixture and then mix.
- Cook for 40 minutes and then decrease the temperature to gas mark 2; 150C and cook for another 30 minutes.
- When cooked, let it cool before eating!

Misha Perrot-Barnaby - Yr.10

The Mysterious Missing Food

Dear Diary,

The other day was so tragic I am just going to remind you of the story.

What happened yesterday was... On a thunderous, stormy night, I came home late from my friends' party, my tummy mumbled and grumbled. I remembered I hadn't eaten anything since the party because they would only let the people who paid for the party have the food. However, I was so hungry that I secretly snatched one rainbow cupcake and saved it until I got home so I wouldn't get caught. Anyway I was too tired to eat I left it until the morning. It's morning time and I have too many things to do so I left it until nightfall and it was midnight and I snuck downstairs secretly and quietly opened the fridge door and my cupcake was GONE! I was so frustrated, that I didn't notice the trail of rainbow crumbs leading to the garage. I eventually noticed it but then when I got to the garage I saw a dark shadow in the corner and heard someone scoffing and munching. I shone a torch light in the corner and saw my dad eating MY CUPCAKE! I started shouting at him and I got another cupcake with HIS money. Later, I went downstairs and opened my fridge door and it was gone AGAIN! And guess who ate it?

Hannah Rawlinson - Yr.7

Reception Class's Oaty Biscuits

Ingredients:

75g (3oz) plain flour
1/2 a level tsp bicarbonate of soda
75g (3oz) Demerara sugar
75g (3oz) porridge oats
75g (3oz) of butter/dairy free margarine
1 tbsp golden syrup

Method:

Put the plain flour in a bowl with half a level teaspoon of bicarbonate of soda.
Add the Demerara sugar and porridge oats and stir together.
Heat the butter in a pan with a tablespoon of golden syrup.
Mix it altogether and roll it into small balls (you should have about 24).
Set them well apart on a greased baking tray and bake at gas mark 3/ 160 C for 20-25 minutes until golden brown.

Reception Class

Yummy Cookies

Ingredients:

- 100g of sugar
- 100g of butter
- 1 tbsp of golden syrup
- 75g of self-raising flour
- Cookie extras (i.e. chocolate chips)
- Another 75g of self raising flour

Method:

1. Pre-heat the oven to 180 degrees.
2. Mix the sugar and butter together to make a paste.
3. Add the golden syrup.
4. Add the first 75g of flour and whatever you are adding to your cookies (i.e. chocolate chips). Mix together.
5. Add and mix the last 75g of flour.
6. Arrange on a baking tray in 10-12 blobs, don't flatten them.
7. Put them in the oven at 180 degrees for 12-15 minutes.

Morgan Creer - Yr.5

Extreme Mini Choco Cheesecakes

I really like this recipe because it is very tasty and delicious. It is a very creamy chocolaty recipe and loads of people like it.

The recipe came about one day when I was bored and started experimenting in the kitchen and it was loads of fun.

The recipe I would say would be in the autumn season.

Ingredients:

- Toblerone chocolate
- White chocolate
- Digestive biscuits

Utensils:

- Bowls
- Microwave
- Mini molds
- Spoons
- Fridge

Instructions:

1. Melt the white chocolate in a microwave for 1:30 minutes and stir continually.
While the chocolate is melting crush some digestive biscuits.
2. Mix the digestive biscuit crumbs and white chocolate together.
3. Then place the mixture into the moulds.
4. Place the moulds in the fridge.
5. While the mixture for the bottom is cooling down you must make the top.
6. You then start to melt the toblerone in a microwave.
7. Keep on stop the microwave and stir it so it does not burn.
8. Take the base out of the fridge.
9. Pour the melted toblerone chocolate into the moulds on top of base.
10. Place the moulds back into the fridge.
11. Wait till the mini cheesecakes have cooled completely.
12. Then take them out and enjoy.

Chloe Phillips - Yr.7

Chocolate Barfi

Chocolate Barfi- poem

Coated with mouth-watering chocolate
Hour by hour intriguing you
Originally from the heart of India
Charming you with its rich, luscious looks
Overwhelmed by the enchanting taste
Licking its lips as it watches your every move
As you bite, every flavour is full of thrill
Tasty temptation of trickling chocolate
Ecstatic shock of sweet delight

Barely able to miss a glance
Addiction for Barfi will haunt you
Round and round the whisk swivels
Fantastic flavours fill your mouth
I love chocolate Barfi.

Description:

My recipe is chocolate barfi and it is an Indian sweet which is eaten everywhere in India on Diwali. This recipe is a scrumptious desert! It is layered with a soft base and on top, melted chocolate. This soon turns hard and becomes a delicious treat for all.

Diwali occurs during the months of October to December depending on the Lunar calender. As it is held in the English autumn I think it best fits this season.

I have chosen chocolate barfi as it is extremely special to me. On Diwali it is a family tradition that we make any sort of barfi: chocolate, coconut, almond or even pink barfi but my favourite is chocolate.

Ingredients:

- 5O grams unsalted butter (and more for greasing)
- 1 heaped tbsp. coconut
- ¼ cup sugar
- ½ tsp. cardamom powder
- ¾ cup milk
- 3 cups milk powder
- 1 heaped tbsp. almond powder
- 4-5 squares chocolate
- ½ tsp. vanilla essence

Method:

- Mix butter, milk and sugar in a microwave casserole and cook on medium for 6 minutes, stirring in between.
- Stir in milk powder, almond powder, coconut, vanilla essence and cardamom and cook on high for 2 minutes then stir.
- Grease a medium size rectangle dish and lay it firmly with a spatula and let it cool.
- In another bowl, melt cooking chocolate in microwave for 30 seconds and stir. Repeat this till the chocolate has melted- make sure you do not overcook.
- Spread it evenly on the barfi. When cold, cut into small equal pieces.
- Keep in the refrigerator until serving.

Tips:

- Prepare barfi one day before, allowing time for sugar to melt.
- Cut the barfi at room temperature to stop the chocolate from cracking.
- Serve at room temperature.
- If the mixture is dry add a little extra milk to make a soft consistency.

Dessert Of Death

A warm breeze flew into Sophie's face as she entered Pizza Hut and smelt the heavenly whiff of lovely pizza. Along with her she had brought her best friend out for dinner- Daisy. Hoping for a table they asked the waiter. The waiter escorted them to a table for two. They grabbed a menu and rapidly began to decide what to eat as they were starving.

Slowly the waiter approached the two girls and took their order. They looked around, Pizza Hut was extremely busy, they decided to order their dessert at the same time as their main.

"We will have some profiteroles please!" said Sophie.

" I forgot to tell you we have this tremendous deal on only today, it's a special double fudge trifle you have to try it , it will make you mouth water, only £4.99!" replied the waiter.

"No thank you we are fine, just profiteroles for dessert" said Sophie sternly.

"No you have to try this you're missing out," said the waiter persuading them to buy it.

"NO JUST PROFITEROLES!" screamed Sophie furiously.

"I'm warning you!" whispered the waiter as he walked away.

As time went by Sophie and Daisy sat patiently despite the little row before. Suddenly Sophie felt a cold finger touch her neck. She jumped!

"Are you alright?" asked Daisy.

Taking a long deep breath Sophie replied "I'm fine." She sat down calmly and wondered what happened. As she sat back she felt a razor-sharp nail dig into her shin and clutch her leg. This sent a bolt of fear down her spine and she froze like a film on pause. Sophie wanted to scream but her mouth was dry and it felt like a rough, wrinkly hand was grasping her throat.

Sophie tried all she could to alert Daisy however, Daisy was too busy texting too even realise a thing. Sophie's eyes were fixed on a mysterious dark figure lingering near the till.

Courageously she staggered to the till, this mysterious figure caught Sophie by the stomach and squeezed her tight. She was petrified. She felt liquid running down her shoulder. She looked at the liquid; it was dark brown almost like fudge.

The figure whispered in her ear:

"I am chocolaty and sweet,
I am such a delightful treat.
You decided not to eat me;
therefore you will never be set free.
For I will haunt you day and night,
I am a tasty trifle, now you will never see the light!"

As the wicked, waiter walked past her. He smiled and muttered "DON'T SAY I DIDN'T WARN YOU..."

Janvi Patel – Yr.7

What Food Will Do To You

Food can make you happy,
Food can make you cry,
Especially when it drops
Straight down to your thigh.

It increases your dress size,
It makes you really fat,
So when you stuff your face
Be sure to think of that.

There are a lot of food groups,
You need to get them all
Or suddenly your blemishes
Will no longer be small.

My favorite is Shepherd's Pie,
A yummy British treat.
I hope that my poem has taught you
To be careful what you eat.

Morgan Adams - Yr.10

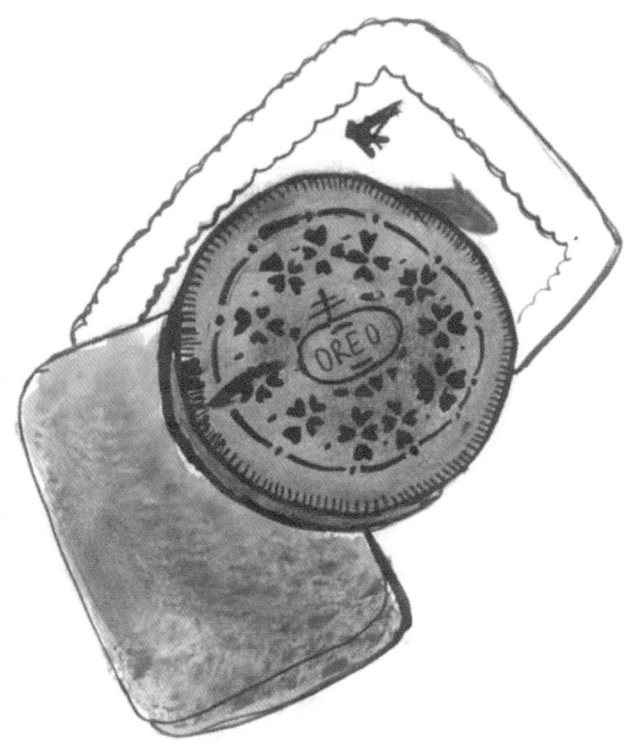

My Beloved Food

I love food
I eat it all the time
I can't help it
I'm just hungry all the time

They can be bitter, sweet, sour
But I know which one I'll prefer
They can be rich, dry, smooth too
But since I prefer sweeter food
I think chocolate soufflés are good

I love food
I eat it all the time
Anywhere, anytime, if possible
I'll try to refrain myself from time to time
But I really don't think it is possible sometimes
Food is my life – take it away and
I'll die

Crunch crack slurp
The crunchy biscuit
The crispy crisps
'Would you like some?' someone asks

Of course I would like some,
But wouldn't it be mean
If I took too much?
Oh well, if I took too much,
They can't complain,
They know I can't say no!
Because I love food so much

Anna Yuen - Yr.10

Apple Pie

Waiting in the kitchen
For mums apple pie
Any body new here,
Can't wait to try.
She serves it with some custard
And maybe cream,
All my family love it,
It truly is a dream.

Tonight is a miracle,
Mum's making two,
I can't wait to swallow it,
But it's not for you.

Imogen Frost - Yr.6

My Short Story

This short story is about my sisters christening party at my house. After the christening party, at the church, all our close family and friends were invited to our house for a party.

It was a buffet party and the food was made by my family. The most popular dish was the Greek meatballs; everybody filled up their plates with them- even the children! It was the most popular dish.

I was waiting patiently for my best friend to arrive at the party- she was an hour late! As I greeted her she said she was really hungry and couldn't wait to eat and have her favourite party dish of meatballs! She hurried to the buffet and started filling up her plate. She asked me where the meatballs were, so I pointed to a plate with only two meatballs left! She was so glad she had the last two meatballs!

Marie Kypreos - Yr.9

Winter

Dinner at the Lords

Thursday 22nd March 1345

Dear Diary,

Yesterday my wife and I went to go eat dinner at the Lord's house. I was quite scared at first... but man... the food was delicious! It was like a feast! As the Lords are very posh (because they're rich) they thought it was rude to dip your fingers into your trencher (a thick piece of bread, you eat your food off) or to wipe your hands on the tablecloth. It is a very different life as a rich person. All the meat we ate wasn't fresh so they had to put lots of spices to mask the flavours of the smoke. The meat was cooked on a spit (a giant barbecue). It was funny because we had to eat with our fingers, the only cutlery there was the knife-like tool called the whittle. The whittle is used for holding or slicing chunks of meats or vegetables. The cups we drank out of were made out of metal or earthenware. The plates were made out of SILVER!! Only very rich people like the Lords would have plates like that. It was absolutely amazing!

We drank wine as well, not ale!

Goodnight Diary.

Shania Devani – Yr.7

Colourful Food

Red is for the juicy berries falling to the ground,
Green is for autumn apples cooking in the pan,
Brown is for the roasted turkey stuffed with sweet pistachios,
Purples for the ripened plums made in Christmas pudding,
Blue is for the lush flowers surrounding the Christmas chicken,
Orange is for the hot tomato sauce boiling in the bowl.
Yellow is for the sparkling wine whirling in the glasses,
Pink is for the cupcake icing topped on chocolate sponge,
Black is for the groovy gravy pouring down the pork,
And white is for the icing on the plump sweet Christmas pudding!

Maddalena De Cesare - Yr.6

Aash-e sholeh-ghalamkar

History of Aash

While rice is the staple, Iranians also eat a lot of legumesand pulses. Lentils are cooked in many soups and stews, often in combination with several types of beans. Aash e Sholeh-Ghalamkar is one example. Aash means soup in Farsi and this is a very rich, stew-like soup.

This dish comes from the north of Iran where the weather is mild and rainy in the winter (similar to England).

They usually make Aash for someone who came back recently from Hajj (home of god); the meat, which they use, to make Aash, is the meat of animal which was sacrificed for god, by the person which went to Hajj. That is why Aash is one of the holy foods.

The Taste Of Aash To Me:

I am in love with this dish because it is specialised for the mild rainy Iranian winter.The fresh, hot, sweet ,golden onions make you think of the warm summer which you are waiting for and the white, cold curd on the super-hot Aash makes you feel the coldness of the winter all the way through your stomach. You can serve Aash with some bread but Aash itself is known as a complete meal.

Ingredients: (4 servings)

- Vegetables, 500 grams each : parsley, dill, coriander, spinach, spring-onion ends.
- 100 grams of long-grain or basmati rice
- 100 grams of peas, beans and lentils
- 500 grams of beef/lamb
- 3 large onions
- 1/2 teaspoon of tumeric
- Cooking oil
- Salt
- Black pepper

Directions:

1. Soak peas, beans and lentils in water for 4-5 hours.
2. Peel and chop onions and fry in oil until slightly golden.
3. Cut meat into small pieces and fry with onions until it changes color.
4. Add peas, beans, lentils, turmeric, salt pepper and hot water, and cook over low heat about one hour .Wash rice and add to the Aash
5. Cook for another 20-30 minutes.
6. Wash vegetables and chop finely. Add to Aash and cook for another 10-15 minutes, stirring frequently
7. Add more hot water during cooking if necessarily.

A Bowl of Aash

The green herbs, make me think of the horrible killers,
The white curd, makes you flew on the rivers,
this amazing meal makes you think of the hell and heaven.
From time immemorial, Aashes and broths have been the worldwide medium
for utilizing what we call the kitchen byproducts or as the French call them, the
'desserts de la table'' (leftovers),
or 'les parties interieures de la bête', such as head, tail, lights, liver, knuckles
and feet.

Beautiful Aash
BEAUTIFUL Aash, so rich and green,
Waiting in a hot tureen!
Who for such dainties would not stop?
Soup of the evening, beautiful Aash!
Soup of the evening, beautiful Aash!
Beau—ootiful Aaaa-shhhhh!
Beau—ootiful Aaaa-shhhhh!
Aashe of the liiiife,
Beautiful, beautiful Aasheeeeee!

Romina Khajoue - Yr.9

Awamat

Ingredients:

- 8 cups of pastry flour
- 1 qt.cup of yoghurt
- 1/2   tsp.of soda
- 1 1/2 cups of olive oil
- Sugar syrup

Preparation:

1. Sift flour and mix with yogurt and soda.
2. Knead together well.
3. Heat olive oil until almost boiling. Put the tbsp of boiling oil onto the dough.
4. Mould the dough into small balls then fry a few at a time. When they quickly rise to the surface and are brown brown, they are ready to be skimmed out of the fat.
5. Drain on absorbent paper.
6. When they are all fried, dip a few at a time in sugar syrup.
7. Serve hot or cold. and enjoy

Awamat is a traditional and common sweet in Lebanon. This is one of my favourite Lebanese sweets because of its syrupy taste. When you bite into each ball the sweet syrup flows out of it into your mouth and it feels like you're in heaven.

This desert can be eaten in all the seasons in a year but preferably winter because if you heat them up the warm syrup and the crunchy outer layer sizzle in your mouth warming you up.

This sweet runs through my family from my Great Granddad up until now and everyone in my family loves to eat it after a nice hot meal. I highly recommend this desert

Nour Borghol – Yr.9

Homemade Flatbread

My recipe is homemade flatbread. I think it is a quick, short recipe to cook and I guarantee you will be satisfied when you have made it. Flatbread is delicious and when you have no idea what to make for dinner try it with some warm soup. It is soft bread just like the Indian bread "naan bread." To make this lovely flatbread even tastier it is topped off with some yummy fresh parsley!

I got this delightful recipe from my cooking classes. We made a variety of foods but I thought the flatbread was a warm and delicious dinner to have on a cold windy day. As it is served with warm soup I think it fits best in winter. Especially when you've been playing outside in the snow when it is freezing cold!

Homemade flatbread is special to me because my mum makes it quite often and I and my sister just scoff the whole plate down!!! I also enjoy the soft fluffiness of the bread as you bite into the flatbread.

Ingredients:

- 55g (2oz) Parmesan cheese, finely grated
- 1 packet (290g) pizza base mix
- 3 tbsps. Finely snipped fresh parsley
- 2tbsps. Olive oil
- About 200ml (7 fl 0z) warm (hand hot) milk

Method:

1. Preheat the oven to 200 oC/ fan 180 oC/ Gas 6.
2. Add the finely grated cheese and pizza base mix together, also adding the parsley. Mix well. Add oil and enough milk, mixing to form soft dough. Knead dough on lightly floured surface for 5 minutes or until smooth.
3. Roll dough out within an inch of the edge of your baking ware. Set aside in a warm place for 15-20 minutes. Prick entire surface with a fork. Cut the dough in 12 pieces and then bake for 15-20 minutes or until deep golden brown.
4. Remove from oven and leave to cool. Break or cut into pieces and serve with warm soup.

Janvi Patel - Yr.7

Recipe for Grandma's Potatoes Latkes

Ingredients (Makes around 15-20):

- ½ an Onion
- 4 or 5 potatoes
- 2 tablespoons of flour
- A pinch of salt
- ¾ of a cup of oil (for frying)

Method:

Wash your hands and your cooking utensils
Peel, wash and chop the potatoes finely
Chop your onion finely
Add the chopped potatoes to the onion to a bowl and mix with a pinch of salt
Now add the two tablespoons of flour and mix well until you come to a type of paste
With the paste take some and mold it into a sort of round shape ready to go in the pan
Put the oil in the pan and turn the gas on a high level
Fry the latkes until they go a golden brown (if they soak up the oil don't be afraid to add more oil)
When finished put them on kitchen roll to soak out the oil
Now they are ready to eat, Enjoy!

Description:

Potatoes Latkes are best known to be eaten around winter time they are very fatty and filling. When eaten warm it gives you a good sensation in your stomach. There aroma is a very oily but heart-warming smell, they make a lovely sizzling sound as if someone has made a snake really angry! Potato Latkes look scrummy. They have a very tanned look about them and no human so far has turned them down. Latkes are known very well in the Jewish religion to appear around Chanukah time to remind them of the oil that was found. They are very irresistible and tasty but to many of them aren't that good for you!

Emily Kenton – Yr.8

Okra

Ingredients:

- Okra – 1 kilo cut into small pieces
- Salt – 1 tablespoon
- Onions – half a kilo finally sliced
- Tomatoes – half a kilo
- Red chilli – half a tea spoon
- Cumin seeds – half a tea spoon
- Turmeric – half a tea spoon

Method:

1. Cut, wash and then dry the Okra.
2. Heat oil in the pan and fry the onions.
3. Add the tomatoes, salt, chilli, turmeric and cumin seeds and fry all for 3-4 minutes.
4. Next add the chopped okra.
4. Cook on a slow fire and stir slightly when required.
5. Serve hot with Nan Bread and slices of lemon.

Afzaa Altaf – Yr.5

Kashke Bademjan

Ingredients:

- 2 large eggplants
- Salt
- 1 tablespoon olive oil
- 1 medium onion, chopped finely
- 2 tablespoons olive oil
- 4 -5 garlic cloves, chopped finely
- ½ cup sour cream
- 1 tablespoon olive oil
- Dried mint
- Salt and pepper

Directions:

Preheat oven to 325 degrees.
Peel the eggplant, and cut a slit along the side. Salt it, and let it sit and drain for half an hour. Rinse salt off.
Slice two eggplants thin lengthwise into 5 or 6 pieces each.
Baste in olive oil on both sides.
Lay these in an oven proof dish and cook them until they are golden brown.
Chop the onion and garlic cloves, and fry them in a pan with olive oil.
Remove the eggplants from oven, add them to onion/garlic mix. Mash the mixture in a food processor or with a spoon until it is chunky but smooth. .
Add sour cream, simmer for fifteen minutes, to the mixture and place it in a serving dish.
In a smaller pan, fry the mint in oil and drizzle it over the eggplant as garnish.

This dish is best served with warm pita bread, fresh herbs, and fresh radish. This is my favorite dish as it has a unique taste, is quite savory, and it is really simple to make.

This dish can be served at any time of the year; however it works best at winter as it is a warm dish. Persian cuisine is as old as Persian history and has served the important role of bringing friends and rivals closer over the years. In the old days, Iranian families gathered around a sofreh which was a table cloth or spread on the floor over a Persian carpet or kilim. The sofreh was and still is the corner stone of Persian cuisine and a place of gathering, laughter, relaxation, and enjoyment.

Negin Mirtorabi – Yr.10

Chef

As a duty of a chef,
It is my job to notice the
Crackle, splat and the smell
Of the chicken.

Listen to the boom, bosh, and bang
and crash of the pots and pans.

Inhale the deep, rich smell
Of the melting chocolate
You hear the drip, drop of
the pouring chocolate.

You feel the biscuit
as it crumbles in your hand.
Hear the snap and the crunch
as you bite into it.

As you bite into it you can feel all
the flavours coming together
in your mouth.

Chloe Phillips – Yr.7

My Favorite Food

Description

My favourite food is called brown pasta; it isn't actually how it sounds though. It is a variation of different flavours added to penne pasta. The sauces make white penne go brown, there wasn't actually a name for it but my sister and I called it brown pasta and everyone liked it and it stuck. Its tastes sweet but also sour and very nice on a cold winter day. It makes a beautiful and exciting sizzling sound when it's in the wok and makes a warm aroma of sweet soy sauce. Even though it is mainly a winter dish, you can most definitely also a summer meal. It reminds me of when I was little because this has been a meal we have eaten for years in our family.

What it means to me

Brown pasta was created by my Dad, he lived on his own and he didn't have much in his cupboards that night. All he had in was penne, soy sauce, olive oil, salt and brown sugar. He just put all these together and made the pasta turn brown, which is why we call it brown pasta. It is something all my family love and we don't have it very often because when we do have it, we all feel that it tastes that little bit more special. My Dad taught my Mum to make it so we could always have it, no matter where we are. My Mum makes it for me when I am either ill or my Dad is away on a business trip because it reminds us of when we have it together. My sister and I have very strong memories of when we were little and would listen to my Dad telling us how he created it. It is very interesting because when my Dad came up with this recipe 16 years ago, he had no idea that it would me a family favourite with the family he had never even met.

Brown Pasta

Ingredients:

White Penne
Salt
Olive Oil
Brown Sugar
Soy Sauce

Method:

Boil the penne for 10 minutes,
Add olive oil to a wok and stir fry the penne,
Add soy sauce and brown sugar; stir fry until the penne is coated and the
sauce has caramelised,
It is then ready to serve.

Brown Pasta

The sweet sizzling it makes in the pan,
The warm feeling I'm dreaming of,
The sound of the little piece of magic,
Being added to the dancing potion,
From the colour of cream white,
To the golden brown,
The sweet yet sour taste,
The combination just works,
But it tastes absolutely wonderful.
Ella Phillips – Yr.8

Meatballs Poem

The recipe we make is our family tradition,
I think you will find it will give you nutrition,
Whenever we have a party and all my family is there,
We would make this dish for everyone to share,
You'll need mince beef, eggs, onions, potatoes and bread,
And also oregano, mint or other herbs instead,
In addition to these there is sunflower oil, salt and pepper to prepare,
And then you will have plenty to share,
Cooking is fun and easy to make,
But first you need to kneed the mixture well to make the round shape,
Then you fry them in oil for 8 minutes to make thirty or if there is a party
maybe even more,
To serve I suggest pitta bread, salad and rice, do this you will simply adore!

Fried meatballs

Ingredients:

- 500g minced beef
- 2 slices of bread (crust removed)
- 1 medium onion
- 2 eggs
- Mint (one teaspoon)
- Oregano (1/2 teaspoon)
- Salt and pepper
- 3 medium potatoes
- Cinnamon (1/2 teaspoon)
- Sunflower oil for frying

Method:

1. Finely chop the onions and then make the bread into breadcrumbs by using a blender.
2. Peel the potatoes and then grate them. Once the potatoes are grated, put them in a sieve and squeeze away any excess water.
3. Mix the minced beef with bread, onion, eggs, mint, cinnamon, oregano, salt and pepper.
4. Knead the mixture well and shape into round balls about the size of walnuts.
5. Then fry them in hot oil for about 8 minutes (4 minutes on high, then medium for another 4 minutes)

The fried meatballs are normally served with Greek pitta bread, salad and chips or rice. We also normally have it with a minty cucumber dip.

Marie Kypreos – Yr.9

Spaghetti Bolognaise

One day, in Italy, there was a young boy called Boccino, who was a Butcher. His shop sold mince, beef, Lamb, and many different types of meat.
Boccino was walking on the streets of Rome, making a mince delivery to an old, frail man called Mr. Nochi.

It was an hour's walk to Mr. Nochi and Boccino was very scared that he was going to be late. You see, Mr. Nochi owns 1/2 the butchers in Rome, so if he didn't like Boccino's meat, he'd be sacked!

Boccino was running as fast as a cheetah, but then bumped into a young maid called Gabriella; she was making a spaghetti delivery to Mrs. Nochi. Mrs. Nochi owns 1/2 the warehouse's in Rome, Gabriella was in the same situation as Boccino.

When Boccino and Gabriella clashed together, their food deliveries went everywhere! They didn't know what to do, so they gathered all the food that haven't been stepped on or splashed onto cars, and took it to Mr. and Mrs. Nochi.

The Nochi's were *furious*! Two complete dishes mixing together, *horrible*! But they didn't want good food to go to waste, so they tried the combined dish. It was delicious, the flavor filled their mouths like a light being turned on in a dark room. The Nochi's thought it was fate! They called it, Spaghetti Bolognaise and told Boccino and Gabriella to set up a restaurant for Spaghetti Bolognaise to be tasted and remembered by everyone.

Spaghetti Bolognaise Recipie

You will need (measure the amounts according to number serving) :

-Beef Mince
-Spaghetti
-Parmesan Cheese
-Tomato Puree
-Italian Peeled Plum Tomatoes
-Chopped onions
-Hot water
-2 Pots
-A Pan
-A Plate
-Cutlery

Dice an onion into little pieces and put them in the pot with some sunflower oil at a low heat. Cook until the onions are clear.
Get a pan, and put some sunflower oil in the pan, let it sizzle. Open the mince and break it up so there are no lumps. Put the mince in the pan at a high heat for 10 minutes, turn the mince to a low heat. Get some Italian peeled plum tomatoes and put them with the onions. Break up the plump tomatoes with your spoon. Get the tomato puree, squeeze a tablespoon of puree into a medium cup of hot water, mix it, pour it into the pot. Bring it to the boil. Add the mince to the sauce, then cook on a low heat for 1/2 hour. Stir occasionally.

Leave the sauce on a low heat once it is cooked. Get another saucepan and put the water in and boil. Once the water is boiled, add the pasta. Cook until soft.

After the Pasta is cooked, Put the pasta on the plate, then the sauce.

Spaghetti Bolognaise

Spaghetti Bolognese is a delicious, juicy treat;
It is a winter dish, which I really love to eat.
It's from the heart of Italy, where Spag bowl's made with care,
To me it is a delicacy, I eat it everywhere.
My parents used to cook it, a lot when I was younger,
And when I eat this food, it always stops my hunger.
The presentation's lovely, welcoming and neat,
Compared to other foods, this dish is hard to beat.

Caity Shaw – Yr.8

Bacon Bonanza

Poem

I can see my dad smiling at me
Gesturing, "Go wash your hands!"
I can see the potatoes cooking, the bacon sitting on my plate, the sprouts are
being boiled.
I can hear the pan sizzling, my dad is whistling
Chips are being cooked
The pot lid is rocking furiously
The sprouts are done
My dad's calling me, "Sit down"
I can smell garlic being fried
The smell of gas
When it's turned on
Mainly it's the bacon
That smell floods the kitchen
I can taste the bacon, very crispy with the same old salty taste
Just nicer
The chips are hard on the outside, soft on the inside
Melts in my mouth
The sprouts are generally amazing but when dad over cooks them
Very soft
I touch the sizzling bacon, burn and scream "OWWW"
The chips feel hard, nice though
Not too hot
The sprouts are greasy so I drop one, pick it up, yell "Five second rule".
Feel the residue of garlic and grease on the sprouts
The bacon is hot and hard and the chips are as usual very nice

This recipe comes from Northern England
This is important to me because it is cooked by my dad who I love very much
and it tastes absolutely brilliant.

Description:

The bacon is the usual pink colour, only slightly darker. The bacon fat is a very dark yellow and brown and it sizzles which makes it look white. As well as the bacon fat, the bacon also sizzles.
It smells wonderful and the best part is the smell which floods the kitchen.
When you hold the bacon it is somewhat hard and extraordinarily crispy.
 However, It burns your hand a little because it's hot. When you bite into it there is a crackling sound which sometimes can be rather loud.
The chips come out of the pan almost completely brown, but there is the tiniest bit of dark yellow. They are sizzling as well and you should never eat them when they come right out of the pan. You only make that mistake once.

When they have finished sizzling pick up one and bite into it.
Oh like a little piece of heaven! The outside is crunchy but the inside is so soft.
It practically melts in your mouth.
The perfect mixture.

Finally you have the sprouts. They are they are the usual green colour but they look quite shiny because they have bacon fat all over them. There are also a few bits of brown on them (this is the remainder of the fried garlic). They are soft and make no sound when you bite into them. There is now a heavy fried garlic smell everywhere. Pick up a sprout and bite into it but be careful they can be slippery. When you bite into a sprout and you get the most wonderful sensation of bacon grease with a hint of garlic. It definitely improves them.

Recipe:

Bacon-
Fry over medium heat until the fat is completely crispy so that when it is cooled it breaks like crisps.
Make sure when you are cooking it is sizzling

Chips-
Microwave a potato for 4 minutes – leave to cool
Remove the skin
Cut in half, length-wise
Slice each half in 2mm thick pieces
Add sunflower oil to bacon fat – in the same amount
Chop up 4 cloves of garlic, in fine slices
Add garlic and potato slices to hot sunflower oil and bacon fat
Fry, turning often until brown all around
Cool on above medium heat

Bacon Sprouts

After serving crispy bacon and crispy chips with garlic, turn pan low.
Cover sprouts in garlic flavoured bacon fat and sunflower oil
Serve!

You can add celery salt to taste
This applies to chips and sprouts

Elli Taylor-Jukes -Yr.8

Curry Mutton

Equipment

- Pyrex Dish
- Small Dutch Pot
- Knife

Ingredients

- 1 lb of mutton
- 2 teaspoons of curry
- ½ a teaspoon of black pepper
- 1 onion
- 1 clove of garlic
- Seasoning
- 2 tablespoons of olive oil

Method:

1. WASH YOUR HANDS!
2. Wash the mutton
3. Cut the mutton into several small pieces
4. Put the mutton into the Pyrex dish
5. Season using; the pepper, curry, onion, and garlic
6. Add the olive oil to the Dutch pot
7. Place the Dutch pot onto the gas at 200°
8. Put the seasoned mutton in the Dutch pot
9. Cover the Dutch pot with the lid
10. Leave the mutton to cook for 40 minutes
11. ENJOY!

Adelle Morgan-Adefarakan - Yr.8

Chicken Curry

Ingredients

- ½ kg of chicken
- 100 ml of onion paste
- 50 ml. of yogurt
- 1 tsp. of coriander (Dhaniya) powder
- 3 to 4 tsp of salt (to season)
- ¼ tsp. turmeric (Haldi) powder
- 1 tsp chilli (LalMirch) powder
- 1 tsp. garlic (Lehsan) paste
- 1 tsp. ginger (Adrak) paste
- 100ml of oil

- 1 to 1½ tsp. salt (as per taste)
- 100 ml. of tomatoes - ground
- 1-2 green chillies -chopped
- 1 tsp garam masala. OR 1 black cardamom (Bari Ilaichi) seeds,
- 2 green cardamom (Chhotillaichi) seeds,
- 1 small stick of cinnamon (Dalchini)
- 10 black pepper corns (Kali Mirch)
- 6-8 cloves of garlic (Laung)
- ¼ tsp. of cumin seeds (Zeera)

Since I was a young girl my mum has always been cooking her families' special tongue tickling chicken curry which has to be my most favourite meal. Not only because it's spicy but creamy at the same time, also because it reminds me of home and family memories. I remember when I was younger she would invite the whole family round and everyone in my big Middle Eastern family would demand for her special chicken curry.
Aisha Mughal – Yr.11

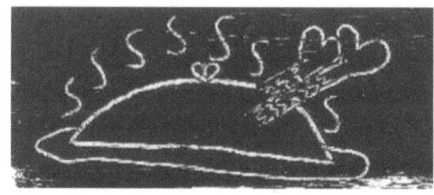

Butter Chicken

Prep Time: 1 hour
Cooking Time: 45 minutes
Total Time: 1 hour, 45 minutes

Ingredients

1 kg boneless chicken (skin removed)
Juice of 1 lime
Salt (for seasoning)
1 teaspoon of red chilli powder (adjust to suit your taste)
6 cloves of garlic
8-10 peppercorns
1 stick of cinnamon
2 bay leaves
Seeds from 3-4 pods of cardamom
1 cup of fresh yoghurt
3 tablespoons vegetable/canola/sunflower cooking oil

2 onions chopped
2 teaspoons garlic paste
1 teaspoon ginger paste
2 teaspoons coriander powder
1 teaspoon cumin powder
1/4 teaspoon turmeric powder
400g/ 14 oz of chopped tomatoes, ground into a smooth paste in a food processor
1/2 litre chicken stock
3 tablespoons soft butter
Salt to taste
Coriander leaves to garnish

Preparation:

Mix the chicken, lime juice, salt and red chilli powder in a large, non-metallic bowl. Cover and marinate for 2 hours.
Heat a flat pan or griddle on medium heat and gently roast (stirring frequently) the cloves, peppercorns, cinnamon and bay leaves until they darken slightly. Cool and add the cardamom seeds. Now grind into a coarse powder using a pestle and mortar.
Mix the yoghurt, your freshly made whole spice powder, coriander, cumin and turmeric powders together and add them to the chicken. Allow to marinate for another hour.
Heat the oil in a deep pan on medium heat. When hot, add the onions. Fry until a pale golden brown in colour and then add the ginger and garlic pastes. Fry for a minute.
Add only the chicken from the chicken-spice mix and fry until sealed.
Now add the tomato paste, chicken stock and remaining part of the

yogurt-spice mix to the chicken.
Cook until the chicken is tender and the gravy is reduced to half its original volume.
Melt the butter in another small pan and then pour it over the chicken.
Garnish with coriander leaves and serve with chapatti bread and black lentils.

For an authentic and traditional cooked-over-the-coals flavour: When the Butter Chicken is cooked, make a small bowl shape with aluminum foil and place it on top of the curry ('floating' on it). Heat a briquette of charcoal on an open flame till red hot and gently put the charcoal in to the aluminum foil bowl. Cover the dish immediately. Remove the cover just before serving, happy eating!

Butter chicken originates from India. I tasted butter chicken for the first time at my Grandma's house when I was ill. The hot creamy sauce trickling down my throat as I tore through the hot soft chapatti.

Vishvitha Talwar – Yr.9

Sausage, Mash and Beans

Here is a recipe for the perfect sausage, mash and bean dinner. One that will remind me of my Grandmother every time I cook it.

1. Heat the oil in a large frying pan, turn the heat to medium and add the sausages. Fry until the sausages are golden brown and firm, turning them from time to time −this should take about 20 minutes. Once cooked, place in an oven-proof dish and keep warm until the mash and beans are ready.

2. Meanwhile start the mashed potato by boiling the potatoes in lightly salted water until soft. Drain, and keep warm until ready to mash.

3. Finish the mash by placing the milk and butter in the pan used to boil the potatoes. Mash using a potato masher. Whip the mashed potato lightly with a wooden spoon. Season with salt and pepper.

4. While serving your meal place the baked beans in the microwave for 3 minutes, so they are served extremely hot.

5. Once the meal is ready, cut all the sausages into small pieces. Spread the mash with your fork and place the beans on top. Squash the beans into the mash until you have a fluffy red mixture. Now place your pieces of sausages on the top. You have now made a Sausage, Mash and Beans castle. Enjoy!

Mikki Adams – Yr.11

Shepherds' Pie

Ingredients:

- Lamb
- Potato
- Carrots
- Swede
- Parsley
- Water
- Olive Oil
- Salt
- Pepper

Preparation

1)Chop the onion and garlic
2) Chop the carrots and swede into small pieces.
3) Chop the parsley.
4)Peel the potatoes, and place them into a pan of salted water.
5)Pour the olive oil into the pan on a medium heat and add the chopped onions and garlic for max of 5 minutes.
6)Add the carrots and swede and cook for a further 5 minutes.
7)Add lamb to the pan and stir until it turns brown.
8)Add the vegetables and parsley.
9)Turn the heat to low and place a lid over the pan.
10)Put the potatoes on a medium heat for 25 minutes until cooked.
11)Drain all of the water from the potatoes and leave for 5 minutes.
12)Spoon the mashed potato gently over the meat and even it out gently.
13)Put the dish in the pre-heated oven and cook for 30 minutes.

Morgan Adams – Yr.10

Beans and Chips

Ingredients:

- Plate
- Beans
- Tin opener (For the beans)
- Chips, or curly fries (But if you want to make your own chips here's the instructions):
    - It's easy to make your own chips; all you have to do is this:
    - Grab a bag of potatoes.
    - Pick out a potato and take out a peeler.
    - Carefully scrape the potato skin off the potato, or you can leave a streak of skin for a nice flavour.
    - Chop the potatoes in a nice shape then put foil over the pan in the oven and drizzle oil all over them.
    - Put the potatoes in the oven for about 20-25 minutes at about 250oC.

Instructions:

1. First grab some baked beans. Open and put it in the microwave for about a minute and half. (This is optional, you can put onions in it!)
2. While the beans are cooking you can put chips in the oven. (You can put any chips in, like curly fries.)
3. Then put the chips on a plate and pour the beans all over them.
4. Add salt and pepper for seasoning

Here's another thing:
You could try Cheese and Chocolate or maybe Chips and Custard!

Hannah Rawlinson – Yr.7

Pork Dumpling

Serves 4 people

Ingredients:

- 500g of minced pork
- 2 leaks
- 2 tablespoons of soyasauce
- 2 tablespoons of rice wine
- 2 tablespoons of sesame oil
- 1 tablespoons of sugar
- 4 tablespoons of potato starch
- 3 tablespoons temmenjan (sweet Chinese miso)
- Rice paper

Method:

- First,put all the ingredients except the rice paper in a bowl.
- Knead it.
- Get the rice paper and hold it as if you are holding a cup.
- Put the things you kneaded in the rice paper.
- Next,put some water in a frying pan.
- Steam on a high heat for 10 minutes.

Suzuna Shibasaki – Yr.5

A Winter Adventure

One winter night, I peered out my window, only to see an Elf! He was the size of a snowflake and he wore a doll sized green costume. He had a grey beard down to his feet. I instantly ran downstairs with my coat and hat to say hello. As I opened the door he hid in a Coke can lying on the floor. I said, "Don't be afraid, I won't hurt you!"

Slowly, he began to slide out of the can. He looked up at me as if I were a giant about to eat him. When I sad hello, I expected him to be quiet, but he was actually a jolly, open little man. I laughed with him and he surprised me by saying, "Since it is so cold, here in England, I can take you on my Elf sleigh to Madagascar!"

I was very pleased with this offer but insisted I was too big to fit in an Elf sleigh. Just then, the Elf remembered he had a shrinking gun in his green pocket. Before I knew it, I was suddenly the size of an Ant! The Elf snapped his tiny fingers and a bright red sleigh flew to the ground straight from Elfia (that's the place where all the Elves live). The clumsy Elf looked around for a map to Madagascar while I threw off my coat and hat because I thought it would be boiling. It turns out that the Elf accidentally pressed the button to Fleland (that's where the enemy gnomes live). Gnomes despise Elves and are always trying to take over Elfia.

Off we zoomed, on a terrifying journey, and crash landed right into some sort of prison. I managed to look at the sign outside and it said 'ELF JAIL'. "Please let me go!" screamed the Elf, "I am the King of Elfia!" I stared at him, and bowed down low to the King. I had no idea he was part of The Royal Elf Family! The doors of the jail opened and the King of Fleland walked in, sniggering at the poor Elf. "Well, well, well if it isn't my dear brother! What are you doing in my Kingdom?" he asked. The Elf didn't say a word. I comforted him but they took me by the hand and pushed me out of prison because I wasn't an Elf!

Then I thought of a plan! I was going to steal a sword and then dress up as an Elf so I'd be thrown back into prison, then we could cut our way out! I smiled to myself happily. I remembered the other Elves in jail too. I would distract the King and open all the cages, and we would squeeze into the Elf sleigh!

So that is what I did! I got thrown back into jail with a sword in my little pocket. The Elf didn't look surprised to see me but seemed delighted when I passed him the little sword and we were both free! The Elf passed around the sword to the other Elves and we all jumped into the sleigh. We flew away from Fleland and everyone was safe.

This was the most eventful winter I had ever experienced.

Feeza Patel and Imogen Frost - Yr.6

Winter Poem

W is for watermelon ice cream in the evening
I is for irresistible chocolate cake
N is for Nutella on toast
T is for a cup of tea for parents
E is for candy filled egg cups, hopefully not for breakfast!
R is for radishes which are certainly NOT tasty!

Imogen Frost - Yr.6

Portakali Revani

The recipe that I have chosen is called "Portakali Revani" which means "Orange Cake" in English. This cake is very scrumptious because it has a sauce which makes it taste delightful.

This recipe is mainly eaten in winter because the ingredients grow at their best at this time of year. The dish is foreign and it comes from the country "Turkey", which is in the middle of Europe and Asia. I'm quite fond of this recipe because it looks very exquisite from the outside and it tastes very delicious from the inside. I find this dish very tasty

Ingredients:

- 3 eggs
- 1 cup of powdered sugar
- 1 cup of semolina
- 2 oranges
- 1 tablespoon of baking powder
- 1 tablespoon of vanilla
- 1.5 cups of flour
- Cooking oil

For the Sauce

- 3 cups of sugar
- 3 cups of water
- Half a lemon

Utensils

- 2 bowls
- Mixer
- Grater
- Baking Tray
- Cooking Pot
- Plate

Method

1. Break the eggs into a bowl.
2. Add in the sugar and mix with a mixer for 5 minutes until smooth.
3. Insert the vanilla, flour, semolina and the baking powder into the other bowl and mix.
4. Put both mixtures together and mix until smooth.
5. Grate the thin sides of one orange and squeeze the juice out of the other.
6. Add these to the mixture and beat thoroughly until smooth.
7. Coat the baking tray with cooking oil and flour. Then pour the mixture into the tray.
8. Heat the oven to 170 degrees and cook for 30-40 minutes.
9. Get a cooking pot and insert the sugar and the water, and mix.
10. Heat on the stove for 15 minutes, and then add the lemon.
11. Heat on the stove for another 5 minutes.
12. Wait until the sauce goes cold.
13. When the cake has cooked, pour the sauce over it.
14. Serve with either nuts or cream.
15. Enjoy!

My Portakali Revani

My lovely sweet cake,
Is wonderfully tasty,
It tastes like orange!

My delicious cake,
Smells delightfully fruity,
It's just like Heaven!

My fabulous cake,
Looks like paradise to me,
So decorative!

Eda Yukselen – Yr.7

Raspberry Ripple Cheesecake

You will need (per cake):

- 125g of butter
- 250g of digestive biscuit
- 1tsp pure vanilla essence
- 450g cream cheese
- 225g caster sugar
- 300g fresh raspberries
- 60g icing sugar
- 400ml double cream

1. Put the biscuits into a bag and crush them, using a rolling pin.
2. Melt the butter in a pan over boiling water.
3. Add the crushed biscuits into the pan and stir together.
4. Line a 20cm cake tin with cling film. Pour the mixture into the tin and flatten it out evenly.
5. Make the raspberry puree by bringing the raspberry and icing sugar to the boil.   After 10 minutes, cool and press though a sleeve.
6. Mix the cream cheese, caster sugar and vanilla essence together.
7. Whip the double cream until stiff, and then fold into the cheese mixture.
8. Spread topping on the biscuit base –use about ¾ of the cheese mixture .Then spoon over ¾ of the puree and swirl it into the cheese cake mixture. Gently spread on the remaining cheesecake mixture.
9. Drizzle on straight lines of raspberry puree .Pull a skewer across the lines for a feathered affect.

I saw this recipe in a book once, and I decide it was too dull for me .I added little bits here and there, and I found myself staring at a rather delicious, yet odd, recipe. Some people would say this is for summer, but I think it is too heavy for summer and much better for winter. I love the way when you slice it, the base crumbles just in the right way. Cheese cake was originally made by the Ancient Greeks.

Yasmeen Louis – Yr.7

Chocolate Cake

Yummy Yummy
In my tummy
My mummy baked a cake,

She put it in the oven
And hope it raised oh goodness sake

She melted the chocolate sauce
And the aroma filled the air
She added essence of oranges, but never ever pears!

As she took the cake out I ran with a dish and spoon
I cried "mummy let me eat some, oh hurry please come soon!"

Feeza Patel – Yr.6

A Cake Story

This happened when my mum and I had just finished making a big chocolate cake. We thought that maybe we should try putting some icing sugar on the top instead of chocolate icing. I still had lots of work to do to so my mum said she would apply the icing sugar. I had just walked into the living room. When the next thing I heard was a huge crashing sound. I ran into the kitchen just to see a huge white cloud. It turns out my mum had dropped the whole jar of icing sugar and half of the sugar had lifted into the air because it was so light. The whole room tasted like a sweet cloud. I couldn't see much but the air had a wonderful sweet taste and smelt fabulous. It was lots of fun but the whole room was covered in icing sugar so we had to do lots of cleaning up afterwords!

Chocolate Cake Recipe

Ingredients:

- 3 Eggs
- Self-Rising Flour (approximately 240grams)
- Butter (approximately 240 grams)
- Caster Sugar (approximately 240 grams)
- 4 tablespoons of cocoa Powder
- 2 tablespoons milk
- Icing Sugar
- 6 Inch Loose Bottom Cake Tin
- Whisk
- 2 Bowls
- Sieve
- Cake Rack

Preparation:

1. Preheat the oven to 160c.
2. Weigh the 3 eggs in their shells and note their weight.
3. Weigh out the same weight of sugar, butter and self raising flour.
4. Whisk the butter and sugar together in a large bowl until pale and creamy.
5. Break the eggs and whisk into the mixture one at a time.
6. Sift the flour and 2 tablespoons of cocoa powder into a separate bowl, then fold one tablespoon at a time into the other mix.
7. Grease the cake tin and pour in the cake mixture.
8. Bake on a middle shelf of the oven for 45 minutes or until firm, then leave to cool on a rack.
9. Whisk 2 tablespoons of cocoa powder with 2 tablespoons of milk until smooth.
10. Add as much icing sugar as needed to make the icing into a paste.
11. Slice the cake into 2 layers, then sandwich together with chocolate icing.
12. Spread the remaining icing over the top of the cake.

Chocolate cake poem

Chocolate cake! Chocolate cake!
It is so fun to make!
When it's done
There's only one
To share with all of us!

Slicing
Icing
Stir and pour
When it's gone we all want more!

Hazel Newman – Yr.8

Chocolate Soufflés

Ingredients

- 2 tablespoons butter (plus more for coating ramekins)
- 1/4 cup granulated sugar (plus more for coating ramekins)
- 8 ounces good quality dark chocolate- chopped
- 7 eggs- separated egg yolks from egg whites
- Pinch of salt
- Melted vanilla ice cream, for serving – optional

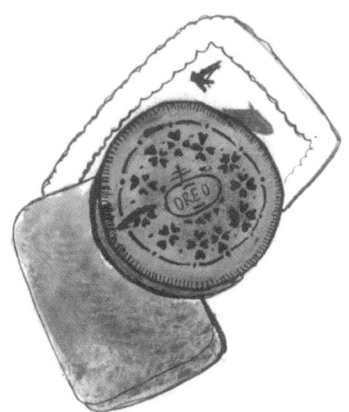

Directions

- Preheat the oven to 350 degrees fahrenheit .
- Butter 6 ramekins or 1 large souffle dish and coat with granulated sugar. Turn the ramekins upside down tap the side of the ramekins to remove excess sugar.
- Heat the chocolate and butter in a glass bowl over simmering water in a double boiler. Stir it occasionally.
- When the chocolate and butter are blended together, remove the bowl from the double boiler.
- Using a hand mixer, beat the egg whites with a pinch of salt in a mixing bowl until soft peaks are formed. Gradually add the 1/3 cup granulated sugar, beating constantly until stiff peaks are formed. In a smaller bowl, whisk the egg yolks until it has a slightly paler color then before. Add the whisked egg yolks to the melted chocolate mixture, then fold in the egg whites.
- Spoon the chocolate mixture into the prepared ramekins and arrange them on to a baking sheet. (To help the soufflés rise evenly, run the tip of your thumb around the inside edge of the ramekins before baking.) Carefully put them in the middle of the oven and bake for about 18 to 25 minutes, they should be risen and cooked.

- Remove the soufflés from the oven and serve immediately; you could serve it with melted vanilla ice cream (in a pitcher, to be poured over the soufflés.)

Other Serving Suggestions

Lightly sweetened whipped cream
A dusting of powdered sugar or cocoa powder

Anna Yuen – Yr.10

Lethal Recipe Book

I sat there, my eyes wide open with excitement, looking at the dusty book before me.

It was unusually big for a book- No not big, grand! It had an almost important air to it and somehow I respected it. It also felt magical, in a queer way, almost alive. I ran my hand over the dusty spine of the book, feeling the engraving along the magnificent, thick, leather cover breathing in the strong book like smell. Then I noticed something, which spoiled the whole effect-there was a red, feeble, half chewed string bound around it.

I must have been there for half an hour or more, but I felt it was it was only seconds. I was intrigued, before I knew I was reaching for the book. The pages were turning. The contents was making my head spin, I felt as if it was dragging me in sucking me up in the words. My ears felt hot and sore and all I could hear was the roaring of my breath. I knew I had to shut the book. I forced myself against what seemed to be a force field and tried to close the book. It took all my might but I managed to close it. Still frightened of what might happen I grabbed the first thing I saw to tie around it and fled, never turning back.

I had tied a red, feeble, half chewed string around it.

Yasmeen Louis – Yr.7

Poem about Chanukah

C is for the Calm feel there is in the room as we light the menorah
H is for the Humming we do while chewing on doughnuts
A is for All the presents that we get
N is for eight Nights of fun and dancing
U is for the Unlimited time you get to spend with your family
K is for the Kosher food we eat and love very much
A is for Aroma coming out the kitchen as my grandma makes the dinner
H is for how Happy we all are.

We eat food fried in oil on Chanukah to remind us of the little bit of oil left in the jug and how it lasted for eight days when it was only predicted to last for one.

Laelle Freedman - Yr.8

Muslim Traditional Foods

Muslims around the world, wherever they are situated, celebrate the Muslim festivals together (depending on the lunar months). However, where you are in the world for the festival generally means the foods you eat during the festival are going to differ from those in other parts of the world.

Traditionally, straight after Ramadan, the first thing a Muslim would eat would be a date which symbolised the breaking of the fast. This is 'breaking of fast' ceremony is called Iftar (Arabic: إفطار).

Caribbean

Iftar is usually held in the social setting of the Masjid. The foods held in the Caribbean for Iftar, reflect the ethnic food eaten in the Caribbean .They have Caribbean food, from roti to goat and duck, and curried chicken to fried rice and aloo (potatoes). Sometimes, depending on the person presenting the meal, there may add non traditional foods to the meal, such as macaroni pie.

Russia

In Russia, dates and fruits are traditionally used to break the fast. Then that is followed by soup and bread and local delights such as khinkal, chudu, kurze, mokhmokh. Then (it is widely believed) the drink kvass is very good to quell the thirst.

Afghanistan
‗
In Afghanistan, is a custom to eat many West Asian foods such as, dates ,shorwa, kebabs, du piyaza, manto, kabuli palaw, shorm beray, bolani, and rice, an dmany, other sweets and delightful deserts.

Every part of the world has its own way of celebrating its festivals, but wherever we are, we all celebrate it together and we all have the same intensions.

Yasmeen Louis - Yr.7

Same Story

I've seen it all before
Same story, even more
But, this time...for once
It's nothing like
I've ever seen before
Gathered again, when
For once, the promises are kept.
No more excuses, no more pain
Ten winters and springs passed
In a blink

Hopelessly,
Running turning twisting
Rushing through the towers
Silver glass
Shining like the sun
Then...
The world ended here
Earthquake of rush
Broke the glassy sun

Sun of eyes, covered
With dark clouds
Rain fell, as she tried
Hopelessly like always

Then, exactly when
Hopes were shattered
In the kingdom of silence
Sun broke its life

Rushing turning twisting, again
Running through the glass
This time joy was host
Earth could not give more

Wooden tree in the middle has seen it all
Just like me
Our laughs, tears, anger and failure
Laughing planning a future
Precious moments
I'll never forget

This dinner
Has to be the most beautiful
The most peaceful on
I've never seen before
I can't believe it
Yet I see it
In them I see Friday
The way we used to be

Negin Mirtorabi - Yr.10

Ruby's Dream

Ruby was sleeping, in her yellow coloured bed. But the way she was sleeping was very queer indeed; she kept twitching her nose, and waving her arms frantically in the air. She murmured in her sleep, and whispered that it was too late; what was going on?

Ruby suddenly blinked open her eyes, and sat up in her bed. She found herself sinking, unable to stop; but she jumped out of her bed as soon as she could, and touched her bed. It was all spongy and porous, just like bread. On the other hand, how could her bed be so spongy when it was made out of wood? Ruby wondered about this for a while, "*Why is my bed so soft? Am I just dreaming, or is this all real?*" she thought.   After a moment of thinking, Ruby came up of what she thought was a solution. It was simple; her bed had turned into bread overnight.

So Ruby thought she had solved the problem and she went downstairs to the living room; where she saw something very peculiar. The colour of the armchair had turned bright pink with rainbow coloured lines on it. As Ruby went closer, she noticed that the rainbow coloured lines where sprinkles and the bright pink colour was strawberry sauce. Ruby thought this was very strange, so she poked the strawberry sauce and put it in her mouth. It tasted just like strawberries. Ruby realised that she was not dreaming, but the furniture had turned into food.

Ruby went to the kitchen and saw that the sink had turned into liquorice. She was getting quite frightened now so she went outside to investigate further. She saw that the grass has turned into apple.

The sky rained blueberry sauce, and the trees had turned into mint chocolate chip ice cream.

Ruby saw a letter on the table:

Hello,
I hope that you have noticed the changes around your house.
The world will stay like this if you don't do something about it. I advise you to

go to your room and shout out "forest!" When you arrive there, I hope you will find me lurking nearby.
Yours Faithfully,
The Big White Sugar Mouse

Ruby wondered who the Big White Sugar Mouse was. She wondered if she should follow the Big White Sugar Mouse's advice. She didn't know what to do. Finally, Ruby went upstairs to her room and hesitated. *Should I shout out forest? Should I listen to what the Big White Sugar Mouse told me?* Ruby thought about it for a while. She had had no other choice, she shouted out "Forest!"...

Ruby opened her eyes, she found herself in the middle of a dark forest. She felt quite petrified and the sight of the forest sent shivers down her spine. Unfortunately, Ruby had no other choice but to find the Big White Sugar Mouse; so she started her journey, looking for the Big White Sugar Mouse.

After walking for 30 minutes or so, Ruby came across a small brook with colourful parrot nearby. She asked the parrot if it had seen the Big White Sugar Mouse.

"The Big White Sugar Mouse, why do you need him?" replied the parrot.
"He advised me to come and look for him," said Ruby.
"Well I saw him this morning. I believe he went to the village," returned the parrot.
"Where is the village?" asked Ruby.
"Oh it is not far from here, it's near the field," replied the parrot.
"Thank you very much Mr Parrot. You have been very helpful to me," thanked Ruby.
"It's alright. If you need any more help please don't hesitate to ask," said the parrot.
Ruby left and walked over to the emerald green field in the distance, hoping to find the Big White Sugar Mouse. After 50 minutes of walking, Ruby finally found the Big White Sugar Mouse. He was a colossal mouse, coated in sparkling sugar.
"Hello, my name is Ruby. Are you Mr Big White Sugar Mouse?"
"I certainly am. If you are here to change the world back to normal, then I advise you to go home."
"Why?" asked Ruby.
"Just go home........"

"Ruby, Ruby! Wake up!" Ruby's mother was saying.
Ruby opened her eyes. *"Where am I"* she thought. *"Where is the Big White Sugar Mouse?"*
Ruby found herself in her room. *Was everything just a dream?* Ruby's mother started calling her again.
"That was the best dream ever" thought Ruby, as she ran downstairs.

Eda Yukselen – Yr.7

Spring

Spring

I love the spring because it is warm.
There are so many pretty flowers that start to grow,
It is very warm and you get bluebells.
The sun shines out, the children are playing.
The animals get babies and they play in the fields.
Easter comes and we get chocolate from the Easter bunny,
Then we get little eggs from friends.
We say thank you and give the eggs too.

Clelia Alishah – Yr.2

An Omelette Containing Fried Rice Recipe

Ingredients (per person):

- 4 oz Chicken
- 1 small onion
- 1 cup part boiled rice
- Salt
- Pepper
- Ketchup
- 2 Eggs

1. Chop the onion into fine pieces
2. Cut the chicken into small pieces.
3. Put the onion, chicken and ketchup in the frying pan and fry.
4. Put part boiled rice in the frying pan. Fry to eliminate the moisture from the ketchup rice.
5. Add beaten eggs to the pan, cook the omelette. Add salt and pepper to taste. Garnish with parsley and ketchup.

Ayuko Yamada - Yr.5

Egg Fried Rice

Egg fried rice is my favorite food. Every-time, I think about it I think of my Chinese family, as it is a Chinese dish. I think egg fried rice is a spring dish as it contains spring onion.

My mum introduced egg fried rice to me, when I was very little. She told me that once she was eating it, I pinched some of the rice and put it into my mouth. It made her very happy that I liked it, as I didn't eat very much when I was young. I love the taste, smell and appearance of it.It tastes so nice and savoury. It smells like Hong Kong in the spring, in the market. It looks so pretty sometimes that I don't want to eat or I will ruin the decoration!

Odayo

Long ago in China a baby boy was born. His name was Odayo. Everything was so happy until there was a loud bang. The door was knocked down and all you could see was a large shadow pulling out a sword. Odayo was too young to realize that his parents were dead and that he had been whisked away by the leader of The Huns. The leader trained Odayo to be strong and brave, as he wanted Odayo to be a Hun.

By the time he was sixteen he was the strongest of them all. He lived only on plain rice. The leader had decided that Odayo was ready for his first attack. Odayo heard the news, and was so excited that he would not let the leader down. They positioned themselves on the top of a mountain with bows and arrows and aimed at a small village. Odayo asked "What are we doing?" "We are going to destroy the village!" replied a Hun, " We are going to kill everyone in China!"

Odayo was frightened and angry, he thought that the Huns were heroes who saved the people of China. That was what the Leader had told him. But he had been taught their ways. He threw his sword down the mountain "Dear me, I seem to have forgotten my sword. May I go get it?"
"Be quick!" shouted the General as he started to sharpen his sword. Odayo walked towards the camp and once out of sight started to run towards the village.
"Run!" he shouted. "Run or you will all be killed!"
"Traitor!" shouted the General "Fire!"

The Huns aimed their arrows at Odayo and started to shoot. Odayo dodged most of the arrows but had been hit in the arm. Odayo managed to stay strong and ran until he reached the village. No one was to be seen. The Huns fled. Odayo smiled and sat down on the floor with his back against a wall. A little girl appeared from hiding in a bush and asked "Are you hurt?"

"Only a little" said Odayo, concerned not to upset her.

She took his hand and lead him to a small house. "Mum! This is the man that saved us!"

"Mimi get some towels for this young man," her mother replied.

Mimi rushed across the house.

"You must be starving" said the woman," how about I make you some egg fried rice?"

"I have never tried egg fried rice" said Odayo, "I have only ever had plain rice".

"Well I'm sure you will love egg fried rice, just like Mimi" said the woman.

Odayo sat down on a chair and soon was presented with rice with bits of yellow in it. Odayo was unsure if he should eat it but he was so hungry he took a big spoonful and popped it into his mouth. Odayo's taste buds started tingling as he tasted savoury for the first time. His nose started quivering as the smell was so lovely. It was like his whole body was happy that he nearly leaped in the air.

"This is amazing!" said Odayo

"Well I am very glad that you like it" said the woman, smiling, "you can stay here a while if you like.

"Thank you" said Odayo.

From that day on Mimi and her parents adopted Odayo and he finally had a family. And then on he was always happy and considered a hero.

Egg Fried Rice Recipe

Ingredients

4 cups of cooked white rice
3 eggs
100g of cooked green peas
One teaspoon of salt
Four tablespoons of oil
Two tablespoons of soy sauce

Method

Beat the eggs together with a pinch of salt.
Heat the third of the oil in a wok and fry the eggs until scrambled.
Transfer them onto a warm plate and break up into smaller pieces.
Heat the remaining oil in the wok and add the cold cooked rice.
Stir well to separate each grain of rice and add the soy sauce and mix until evenly coated.
Add the peas and egg and mix together well on a reduced heat.
Serve straight away and enjoy!!

Egg Fried Rice and Me

Every day and any day I would eat it!
Gorgeous, glutinous rice in a bowl,
Great for eating with friends, not chopsticks!
Fried to perfection in sesame oil,
Rich with flavours and oriental spice,
Infused with soy sauce and peas,
Egg, precooked in a scramble,
Deliciousness in just one bowl!
Ready for dinner and coming home hungry,
I love my egg fried rice!
Cooking in a wok, hot and smoky,
Ever the treat for my Chinese side!

Maya Kan – Yr.8

Tabouleh Recipe

This Tabouleh recipe serves 4

Ingredients:

- 3 cups of finely chopped flat leaf parsley
- 1/2 a cup of finely chopped mint
- 4 or 5 chopped spring onions (with the green parts)
- 4 medium sized tomatoes chopped into small cubes
- 100g of fine burghul
- 1/2 a cup lemon juice
- 4 tbsp. of olive oil
- Salt and Pepper

For the ultimate Tabouleh dish, follow these simple instructions:

Soak the burghul in cold water for 1/2 an hour, then drain.
Mix all the ingredients together and then taste and adjust seasoning if needed.
Serve with lettuce leaves and enjoy

** Important **
When using fresh vegetables and herbs, make sure they are washed thoroughly and drained.

Tabouleh is a simple, tasty, delicious and nourishing traditional salad originally made in Lebanon. It is eaten with any type of food, at any time in the day, in any season of the year. This is a traditional recipe that runs down the family for tens and hundreds of years. It is a juicy, mouth-watering salad. The sour juice from the organic lemons leaves your mouth tantalizing. I personally love eating this salad alongside my main course because it adds a lot of flavour and colour to my food.

Nour Borghol – Yr.9

Warak Enabbel Zait

Ingredients:

500 g (16 oz.) grape vine leaves
4 cups (4 bunches) finely chopped fresh parsley
¼ cup finely chopped fresh mint
½ cup short grain rice
1 kg (32 oz.) finely chopped tomatoes
1 tsp. salt
A dash of allspice
1 cup olive oil and vegetable oil mixture
2 medium onions, finely chopped
3 cups water
2 medium potatoes, peeled and sliced into rounds
¾ cup lemon juice
1 tsp. pomegranate thickened juice (optional)
A dash of ground cinnamon
A dash of ground white pepper

Method:

Filling:

Rub the onions with salt.
Mix rice with onion, mint, tomato and parsley.
Stir in ½ quantity of lemon juice, ½ quantities of olive oil, salt and spices.
Snip off vine leaves stems if necessary.
Rinse in cold water.

Wrapping:

Place a vine leaf (shiny side) down on work surface.
Then, place about a tbsp of stuffing near the stem end.
Fold the end and sides over stuffing and roll up firmly. Repeat the same process with all the other leaves.

How to cook it:

Place ½ cup oil in a heavy pan.
Line the base of the heavy pan with potato rounds and pack vine leaves rolls close together in layers.
Reverse a heavy plate on top to keep rolls in shape during cooking.
Add ½ cup of lemon juice, pomegranate juice, fillings stock and 3 cups of water.
Cover; bring to a boil over moderate heat. Reduce heat and let them simmer for one hour or until tender.
Serve cold garnished with potato slices and enjoy J

Warak EnabbelZait is one of the best Lebanese foods for me! I love eating this food especially when my grandma 'Huda' makes it as she is an amazing cook and she makes these incredibly!

You can eat this food as a starter before any meal because it compliments everything as it is healthy, tasty, and flavoursome. Thinking about it leaves your mouth-watering!

Nour Borghol – Yr.9

German Potato Salad

You will need:

- 500g new baby potatoes, Halved
- 1 medium Onion, chopped
- 1 medium Apple, peeled and chopped
- 10 Cornichons
- 1 tbl low fat mayonnaise
- 1 tbl low fat yoghurt
- ½ tbl pijon mustard
- ½ bunch fresh parsley, chopped
- To taste salt and pepper

What to do:

1. Boil the potatoes
2. Whilst the potatoes are cooking, prepare the marinade with the remainder ingredients. Mix it all together in a bowl.
3. Add the potatoes once they have cooled. Give it a good, but gently stir!

Guten Appétit!

Clelia Alishah – Yr.2

Maru Bhajja

Originally from East Africa (Kenya, Uganda and Tanzania)- mostly coastal regions. I like this dish because it's both a snack and a dish.

Ingredients:

- 500g potatoes- peeled and sliced into thin rounds
- Ginger- grated
- 1 cup gram flour (besan flour)
- Dania- finely chopped
- 4 tea spoon green chillies- crushed
- Tomatoes
- Carrots
- Vegetable oil for deep frying
- Salt to season
- Pinch of bicarbonate of soda

Method:

Mix the ginger and green chillies with the potatoes. Sprinkle them with the gram flour until all the potatoes are evenly coated.
Set aside for half an hour (don't sprinkle any water on the potatoes as the water from the potatoes will marinate everything sufficiently.)
Add the dania to the potatoes and mix well. After half an hour add some salt and the bicarbonate of soda.
Heat the oil in a deep pan and fry the bhajias until golden brown.

Angela   Macharia – Yr.9

Goat Biryani

This recipe is originally from India. My Grandmother taught me how to cook this dish when I was 9 years old. It is my best dish and we normally eat it at celebrations. Whenever I eat or cook this dish I remember my Grandmother and the good memories we had and shared.

Ingredients:

- 500g goat meat
- 1 small green pawpaw
- 8 cloves
- 10 cardamom pods
- 6 sticks of cinnamon
- 2 teaspoons garlic - crushed
- 2 tablespoons cumin seeds
- 8 peppercorns
- 1 bunch of coriander- chopped
- 1 Teaspoon of ginger- crushed
- 2 tea spoon chili powder
- 1 table spoon paprika
- 250ml maziwalala
- 250g tomatoes, chopped
- 3 table spoon tomato puree
- Salt to taste
- 250g onions, thinly sliced
- 1 table spoon turmeric
- Vegetable oil for shallow frying
- 500g rice

Method:

Grate the pawpaw and cut the meat into pieces, set aside. Pound the cloves, cardamom, cinnamon, garlic, cumin, coriander, ginger, peppercorns and chili together. Mix these spices together with the meat, pawpaw, lala, tomatoes, paprika, tomato puree and salt. Marinate for a few hours. Heat the oil and fry the onions until they are brown and crisp. Remove them from the oil and set aside. In the same pot, fry the meat mixture, simmering it until the meat is done. In the meantime cook the rice as usual. Place the meat mixture in an oven proof dish and spread the fried onions over the meat.Place the rice over the onion and meat and spread evenly. Sprinkle some water into the dish and place in an oven at 200 degrees centigrade for 10 minutes.

Angela   Macharia – Yr.9

Peanut Butter Chicken

My mother cooks this dish all this time. I love it because you wouldn't expect a savoury food to go with such a sweet thing.

Ingredients:

- 2 tablespoons of vegetable oil
- 1 lb of skinless, boneless chicken breast halves - cut into 1 inch cubes
- 1 medium onion- sliced
- 7 fresh mushrooms- sliced
- 1/8 teaspoon red pepper flakes
- 1 (14.5 ounce) can diced tomatoes with juice
- 3/4 cup chicken stock
- 3/4 cup smooth peanut butter
- Salt and pepper to season

Instructions:

Heat the oil in a large skillet over a medium heat. Add the chicken pieces, and cook until the chicken starts to turn white. Add the onion, mushrooms, and red pepper flakes. Season with salt and pepper. Cook, stirring constantly until onions are translucent (about 5 minutes).
Pour the tomatoes and chicken stock into the skillet. Simmer for about 10 minutes, or until chicken is cooked through. Stir in peanut butter, and cook stirring constantly until the sauce thickens (this should only take a minute or two.) If the sauce is not thickening stir in more peanut butter.

Layla Pratt – Yr.11

Loubia Polo

This is a rice dish that originates from Iran. It is made from lamb, beans and many different spices.

My mother first introduced this dish to my sister, father and I when we were quite young; now most of my dad's family always request it at family dinners. It was first my Grandmother that taught it to my mum and auntie and they hope to pass it on to us!

The good thing about this dish is that there isn't a certain time of year where you have to eat it, it works all year round and always tastes scrumptious!

The thing I love most about this dish is even if I am in my room and my door is closed I can always smell the different flavours wafting through the house.
This is a comfort dish, even though the preparation and making it does take a while. It is a delicious dish and all that work becomes worth it as nothing can go wrong when making.

Ingredients: (serving for 4-6 people)

- Cut green beans
- Stew meat — use less than .5 lbs, you will want to chop the meat into little pieces
- 1 full tablespoon of tomato paste
- Lemon juice
- Salt/pepper
- Turmeric
- 1 medium onion — finely chopped
- Oil
- 1 1/2 to 2 cups water
- 3 to 3 1/2 cups rice

Method:

First wash your rice and soak it in water.

In a pot heat up some oil and add your chopped onions to it. Once the onion begins turning a golden colour and becomes tender, add your meat to the pot. Stir around the meat and then add turmeric, salt, and pepper. Add your green beans to the pot and allow them to fry a bit. Add water to the pot, followed by tomato paste and lemon juice. Place the lid on the pot and allow the mixture to cook on a medium heat- approximately 1 hour. You will know the mixture is ready when it has thickened and gives out oil.

Once the Khoreshte Loubia is ready in a different pot heat up water on high heat to prepare the rice. Once the water comes to a boil, pour out the water the rice has been soaking in. Pour the rice into the pot of boiled water. When the rice is cooked, use a strainer to strain the rice. In the same pot add some water and some oil. Place it back on the stove top on a high heat. (At this point if you wish to have tahdig sibzamini you can place cut potato slices on the bottom of the pot- wait until the oil is heated before doing so).

Add half the rice into the pot then pour a layer of the Khoreshte Loubia onto the rice. Add the remaining rice and add any remaining Khoreshte Loubia on top; you can mix around the contents a bit and then place a towel over the lid of the pot and cover the pot.

Once the steam begins escaping the pot you can turn the stove top heat to a low temperature. You may want to wait a bit longer before turning the heat to low if you are using potato slices. Let the Loubia Polo cook for 1 to 1 1/2 hours Serve and enjoy!

Amber Codron – Yr.9

Must-o-Khiar

This is a really delicious, healthy and simple dish I especially love in the summer. Many cultures have a yogurt and cucumber dish, but I like the fresh herbal notes in this one. *Persian Yogurt-Cucumber Dish, AKA 'Must-o-khiar'*

Ingredients:

- 2lb tub of plain, unsweetened, unflavoured yogurt
- 2-3 small Persian cucumbers OR 1 regular cucumber
- 3-5 pinches of dried, crushed mint(or more to taste)
- Half tsp of salt or more to taste
- Dash of pepper to taste
- 50g chopped walnuts
- Hand full of raisins(or less)
- Rose petals(optional)

Instructions:

Dice cucumbers into small pieces about ¼ inch square (if using regular cucumbers, seed them and salt them a little to draw out a little water, then rub salt off and pat dry).
Gently squeeze excess water from the cucumber and mix into the yogurt. In a medium bowl, add the yogurt, cucumber, walnuts, mint, salt and raisins. Stir well to combine. Transfer onto a serving dish. Lightly sprinkle with dried mint and dried rose petals.

VOILA, your beautiful dip is now ready to eat and enjoy!

Rosa Soleymani – Yr.10

Little Salad

Ingredients:

The quantities of this salad depend on how many people feeding
- For every half cucumber you will need 3 tomatoes, 2 bottom halves of spring's onions
- Olive Oil
- Salt
- Arabic Vinegar

Instructions:

Wash the tomatoes cucumber and onions.
Chop the tomatoes into little pieces, do the same to the onions and cucumber.
Peel the skin off the cucumber then cut using the grid method. Cube your cucumber by slicing it horizontally and vertically, slice downwards.
Then by tasting it is your decision how much salt, vinegar and olive oil to add.
(This dish is all about personal preferences.)

The reason this dish is called little salad is because it is salad and everything is chopped into little pieces.
This dish is very refreshing and is lovely to have in the summer. It tastes great as a side dish to a barbecue to be shared with friends and family.

Mariam Haddad – Yr.9

Coconut Chutney

My wife lives in South India and this is one of her specialities. It is especially delicious when served for breakfast with tea and a dosa or uttapam (wonderful Indian pancakes). It also works very well as a cooling accompaniment to any curry.

Ingredients:

- 1 cup grated fresh coconut
- 1 chopped green chilli (deseeded, or with the seeds if you like it hot!)
- 1 teaspoon coriander powder
- 1 teaspoon cumin seeds
- 3 cloves of garlic, crushed
- 1 heaped teaspoon ginger paste
- 1 tablespoon white poppy seeds
- 1 dried red chilli
- 1 teaspoon black gram lentils
- 1 handful of curry leaves
- 1 tablespoon vegetable oil

Instructions:

1. Mix the coconut, green chilli, coriander, cumin, garlic and ginger paste. Blend until these make a very fine paste, adding a little water.

2. Fry the poppy seeds, red chilli, black gram lentils and curry leaves in the vegetable oil for a minute. Take care so that they do not burn.

3. Stir the tempered spices and black gram lentils into the coconut mix and serve.

The chutney will keep well in the fridge for a few days if covered.

Mr. Wilson – Music Teacher

The Passage

The slow movement of wildlife
Is a culminating crop that everybody's?
Responsibility relies on,
From the lowly, grey rabbit creeping
out of its
Mothering burrow to
Meet the fateful aroma that nature
possesses
To the average human dustbin,
Snatching and writing for the red and
yellow packaging
Devouring each McDonald and KFC's
one
By one.

Many believe that the cycle of life
Is an old wives tale,
But others faithfully bound themselves
to
The eternal fire of the survival of the
fittest

Is it really the fact that we are all part
of the carbon cycle?
Or is it the Darwinist theory
Just a myth beyond the far realm of life

The meaning of existence
In whose cacophony is
By far the loudest,
Yet in the attempt to
Stifle the incessant habble babble are
Met with disappointment

From father time to Mother Nature
Whose grasp is as icy as death,
Their stare as fiery as hatred
And their breath as sharp as the
northern wind
And whose spouse are who adapted to
the
New and dazzling modern world

And are role models thought,
By our fore fathers
In a quest to find the truth.

Are we who we really are?
Or are we the images of superiority
held
Above us for our reputation to slowly
Crash down?
Did we really hunt the animals for
Our thriving hunger and their
Blood red meat, or was
It horseplay?

Do we really need to violate the
animals
That we take for granted?
Or do we
Care and respect them
For them to become part of us in the
natural food chain –
To eat or be eaten –
To whatever religion or faith
We believe in?

Amelia Rawlinson – Yr.10

Mixed Berry Pancakes with
White Chocolate Drizzle

Ingredients:

- Pancake
- 100g flour
- 2 eggs
- ½ pint milk
- pinch salt
- Strawberries
- Raspberries
- Blueberries
- White Chocolate Sauce
- 50g white chocolate
- 25g icing sugar
- 12.5g unsalted butter
- 15ml water

Method:

Pancakes – Sieve the flour and salt into a bowl. Make a well in the middle and add the eggs. Stir then slowly add the milk, beating the mixture constantly to ensure it is a smooth consistency. Heat a tiny amount of oil in a frying pan. Add some of the pancake mixture so it coats the bottom of the pan. When pancake starts to brown turn (or flip!) and cook the other side. Serve on a dinner plate. White chocolate sauce - Break up the chocolate and put all the ingredients into a heatproof bowl and stand over a pan of gently simmering water, stirring with a wooden spoon until all ingredients are melted and a smooth sauce is formed.

Serving:
Chop strawberries and place, along with raspberries and blueberries, onto the pancake. Drizzle sauce over the fruit and serve. Enjoy!

Helen Stammers - Staff

Cheesecake

Dear Grandma,

Today I tried the most marvelous cheesecake it was so yummy I ate the whole piece of it- that is so unlike me!
I shall send you the recipe for the cheesecake, Nicky nicely gave it to me.
This week I have been trying the most interesting foods because in school it is European week and people bring in all different types of food for classmates to try, you would be surprised with some of the things I have eaten.
I hoped you liked your Birthday present.
I used the money that you sent me for my Birthday and I bought a Shamballa bracelet!

See you soon.

LOTS OF LOVE CHLOE XXXX

Recipe

This recipe is a traditional chilled cheesecake and is perfect for the summer. This recipe came around when me and my dad where making a cheesecake from bits and bobs at home and it is the perfect creamy beautiful recipe to fulfil your needs.

Serves 7

Ingredients:

- Soft cheese
- Double cream
- Vanilla extract
- Icing sugar
- Digestive biscuits
- Butter

Equipment:

- Whisk
- Microwave
- Rolling pin
- Freezer bag
- Spatula
- Baking tin

Method:

1. Crush some digestive biscuits in a freezer bag.
2. Melt 5 tablespoons of butter in the microwave for preferably 30 seconds.
3. Take the butter out the microwave and mix in with the biscuit crumbs.
4 Place the biscuit base in the fridge.
5. Mix together 600g soft cheese, 100g icing sugar, 285ml double cream and a drop of vanilla extract.
6. Mix well till smooth
7. Take the base out of the fridge.
8. Pour the topping onto the base
9. Put it back into the fridge and wait till chilled (1 hour).

Chloe Phillips – Yr.7

New York Cheesecake Recipe

Ingredients:

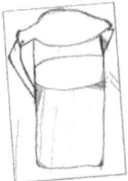

1/3 cup butter, melted
1 1/2 cup cinnamon graham
cracker crumbs
3 1/4 packages (8 oz. packages)
cream cheese, softened
1 can 14 oz. sweetened
condensed milk
2 tsp. vanilla extract
2 eggs

Method:
1. Preheat oven to 300 degrees F. Combine graham cracker crumbs and butter; press evenly on bottom of 9 inch pie pan.
2. In large mixing bowl, beat cream cheese until fluffy. Gradually add sweetened condensed milk, beating until smooth.
3. Add vanilla and eggs, mix well. Pour into prepared pie pan.
4. Bake for 1 hour, turn off oven but leave cheesecake in oven with door propped slightly open for an additional hour.
5. Refrigerate at least 6 hours until firm.

Hannah Garner – Yr.11

My Strawberry Sundae Story

One quiet day in Stillcot village, well.....it wasn't really quiet, because there was a party going on. This party made most of the village shudder and vibrate with the beats of music playing at hillside manor. Hillside manor was the place where the party was taking place, at first look it looks like a normal party, but soon some tragedy will strike the party.....

Lily Little was one of the guests invited to this party, Lily is a 14 year- old girl who has a passion for ridding and loves to eat sweet foods. Lily only came to the party because her parents were friends to the owner of hillside manor. Lily was bored at this party; she was the only child there and she had to pretend be posh. Lily was sitting by the window looking glum as ever, and then a waiter came over to her and asked her if she would like a sweet treat before dinner? The sweet treat was a strawberry sundae. Lily's favourite. Lily thought about what her mother would say to her right now "Lily, your dinner will be ready soon!" but Lily couldn't resist the temptation and took the sundae from the tray.

Lily put a spoon into the sundae and put into her mouth, the taste was sweet and the texture was smooth and creamy. Lily believed she was in heaven.

Later that evening, Lily was meant to be singing to everyone at the party. Unfortunately she felt sick and wobbly. She tried to tell her mother that she didn't feel well, but her mother didn't believe her. As she got on stage, her skin started to go green, she got horrible spots all over her body, and blood trickled from her ears and corners from her mouth. Everyone was speechless and women started to scream, when suddenly she died on stage and turned into a strawberry ice cream sundae.

So next time you're offered a sweet treat before dinner, think twice........

Strawberry Sundae

Ingredients:

- 3 digestive biscuits
- 6 large scoops of strawberry ice cream
- 1 200g bar of milk chocolate
- 8 blueberries and raspberries
- 1 cocktail umbrella (optional)
- 1 glass

Recipe:

1: Crush the biscuits into tiny pieces. Pour into the glass.
2: Put 3 scoops of strawberry ice cream on top of the biscuits in the glass. Smooth down flat.
3: Melt the chocolate down to a liquid form. Once this is done leave it to cool and only then pour on top of the biscuits and ice cream.
4: Put the rest of the ice on top of the chocolate and then smooth it down flat.
5: Lay the fruit on the top of the sundae. Add the cocktail stick.

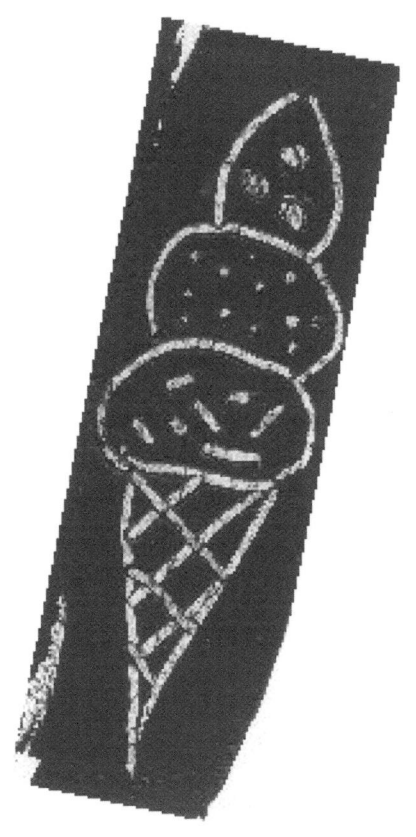

Rachel Price – Yr.7

Robert Steven's Last Supper

It took Robert at least an hour to finish that strawberry sundae. Once at home, Robert regretted eating it. Robert usually ate all of his dinner, but that day he could hardly eat a mouthful. His mother and father were both very angry because it was a waste of food. But they soon stopped and stared at Robert.

Robert's skin had started to go very pale, as pale as milk, then his fingernails grew longer and shaped into little daggers, his clothes became grey and dusty and his face had 3 pinkie-yellowy boils on it. Robert had turned into a mini figure of the ice cream parlor man!

His mother screamed, his father's jaw dropped. Robert was speechless, he thought how this could have happened and then remembered about the strawberry sundae, the man had given him in the shop.

Robert told his mother and father everything, but they didn't believe him. Robert was sent straight to his room until they could get hold of a doctor.

Once in his room Robert kept starring at himself in the mirror, until the ice cream parlor man appeared in the mirror, Robert asked "Why did you do this to me" the man laughed an evil laugh and with that disappeared.

Robert was left feeling confused and ugly. "I wish I could die so I wouldn't have to see myself anymore." He didn't really mean that, but 3 seconds later, Robert dropped dead onto the floor.

So next time you buy an ice cream sundae, think about what might happen TO YOU...

Rachel Price – Yr.7

Raspanilla

Raspanilla is a recipe I made one day. It is basically Vanilla ice cream with raspberries. It is special to me because I love the way the flavours combine to make one gentle, yet delicious flavour.

This recipe is normally made with vanilla ice cream, but can be made with strawberry cheesecake ice cream.

The Chinese have been said to have first discovered ice cream, as far back as 3000BC, however the more recent creators I except most people to be more familiar is with the Italians.

My recipe is simple, yet delicious.

You will need:(per serving)

- Vanilla ice cream (strawberry cheese cake)
- 8 raspberries
- Raspberry jam

Instructions:

Defrost your ice cream. Get your raspberry jam and dollop it into your ice cream cup. Smooth it out until it is only an inch and a half from the bottom of the cup.

Take about 4 of the raspberries and cut them up into little pieces . Mix the ice cream and the chopped up raspberries into the ice cream. Stir until the raspberries are completely submerged in the mixture. Place this on top of the raspberry jam and smooth it down. Finally grab the remaining raspberries and scatter on top of the finished ice cream.

A Raspanilla Limerick

Raspanilla is a lovely food,
To eat it you must be in a good mood,
You must say thank you after,
And please before,
Or it will think you are being awfully rude.

A rather young baker name Roo,
Got fired, and shouted he will sue,
Cried the manger don't shout,
He'll give fifty pounds or about,
Or the rest will want some too.

Yasmeen Louis – Yr.7

A Messy Surprise

Pots and pans,
Spoon in my hand,
Eggs on the ceiling,
Flour on the floor,
My hands are covered in the gloopy mixture I adore.
I stir and mix until it's just right,
More milk, more sugar;
It's really putting up a fight.

'Oops, a little spill there, oh well, I'll do it later.'
I said with no care.
My apron covered in the mess,
The kitchen looks like a bomb has gone off,
Ingredients everywhere, there is no time for cleaning up or rest.

I placed it in the oven, 180 degrees celsius,
ready to be cooked.
'Phew, it's over!'
I sit next to the oven and look.

My mother comes home,
Drops her shopping bags and her jaw.
I stand there grinning;
'I made it for you!'
She tries to smile.
'That's...uh, nice'
She looks around the kitchen for a while.
'I don't understand, don't you like the cake you see?'
'No, I do!' she replied.
'Just next time leave the cooking to me!'

Misha Perrot-Barnaby - Yr.10

Dates cooked in Honey

This dessert is delicious, divine and will tingle your taste buds. You will keep coming back for more.

Ingredients:

- 12 fresh Dates*
- 12 half Walnuts
- 4 tablespoons Honey
- salt
- Black pepper

(* If you can't get fresh Dates then a packet of cooking Dates will do)

Method

- Peel the Dates and remove the stones.
- Substitute each stone with a half walnut.
- Sprinkle each Date lightly with salt.
- Melt the honey in a pan and gently cook the dates in the honey.
- After cooking for five minutes, take out the dates and display in a serving dish.
- Spoon more honey over the hot dates.
- Cover with a little black pepper and serve.

Lucy

Gateau au Chocolat

Ingredients

- Chocolate 50g
- Double cream 50g
- Butter 60g
- Egg yolk (3 eggs)
- Caster sugar 65g
- Meringue (white of an egg)
- Caster sugar 65g
- Cocoa powder 25g
- Weak flour 20g
- Powder sugar (as suitable amount)

Instructions:

- Put chocolate, double cream and butter together.
- Put under cling film to microwave for   1 min and mix with spoon.
- Put meringue and caster sugar in a small bowl.
- Mix cocoa powder and weak flour with 1.
- Preheat the oven (200°c).
- Put cooking sheet inside your circle mould.

How to bake:

1. Mix white and sugar with a whisk.
2. Whip the chocolate, cream and butter.
3. Put cocoa powder and the flour through a sieve. Whip with the mixture.
4. Put 1/3 of meringue and yolk in a bowl. Whip it gently.
5. Mix all the mixtures together, but DO NOT let the bubbles disappear.
6. Pour it in the mould and bake for 15 minutes at 200°c then for another 5 minutes at 160°c.
7. Take the cake out of the oven and let it cool down.
8. Sprinkle the powder sugar over the cake.
9. Dish up with whipped cream.

The reason why I like it is it's a delicious cake and my Mum has baked it before.

Yui Kojima – Yr.5

Mud Pie Pudding

You Will Need:

- 1 Large Bowl
- Clingfilm
- Electric Whisk
- A Fridge
- Caramelized Condensed Milk
- Whipping Cream
- Tea Biscuits
- Flake Chocolate

Method:

Start with a large bowl and very briefly whisk the cream.
Begin to add the Caramelized Condensed Milk whilst whisking.
Break the tea biscuits into bit size pieces and mix.
Break the flake chocolate over the top.
Cover with cling film and put in the fridge.
ENJOY!

This recipe is special as my Gran always makes it for special occasions and it is being passed down to the family.

Madison Creer – Yr.8

The Red Daffodil

Once upon a time there was a daffodil which was red. The other daffodils in her meadow were yellow. The other daffodils sneered at her and made her feel embarrassed. 'I bet she wishes she was yellow like us.' They would whisper in little groups.

Sometimes people would come to walk in the meadow and they would laugh at the little daffodil too. One day a little girl visited the meadow with her father. The little girl was so small she couldn't see the red daffodil through the crowd of people looking so her father lifted her up on his shoulders.

'Oh, what a beautiful daffodil, how lucky it is to be different from other daffodils!' exclaimed the little girl in wonder. The other people heard her.

'Do you know I was thinking that myself' they whispered to each other. The red daffodil blushed from all the attention, the other daffodils however weren't very happy.

'How silly these people are' muttered a scrawny old daffodil.

'I couldn't agree more darling' a slender bloom replied.

It so happened a Princess heard about the red and popular flower and came to see it herself. "Take my dog out of her cage and let her into that meadow". She said to her servant. The servant was bewildered but did as he was told. The dog plucked the red daffodil out of the meadow. He didn't hear the red daffodil utter a sigh. Although, the flower had been so terribly unhappy, it also knew it was about to leave the only home ever known it. The flower wondered what the future held.

The red daffodil was laid gently in a basket of wicker filled with other beautiful flowers. There were poppies, roses, lilies, tulips and pansies. Every single one of them was a gorgeous red! The red daffodil felt dazed, but also excited and welcomed.

The flowers travelled with the princess in her coach, all the way to the palace. On arrival she asked the flowers what was going to happen to them.
"Dont you know?" said a practical poppy. "We are going to be made into a

stunning heavenly bouquet for the Princess Scarlett and the Prince Crimson wedding"

It was a stunning wedding and the flowers enjoyed it very much. After the wedding, the princess threw the red flowers onto the royal garden, where they led a lovely, new life, so they were very happy.

Phoebe Brady – Yr.5

Summer

To Make My Favorite Meal

My Starter is called:

Fruit Salad

Ingredients:

Any selection of fruit you like

Cooking Instructions:

1. Wash all of your fruits under cold water
2. Cut them all up into cube shapes of similar sizes
3. Then put it into a bowl (eat immediately or chill until ready to eat)

My Main is called:

Dodo

Ingredients:

2 Plantains per person
Vegetable oil or sunflower oil
Salt (optional)

Cooking Instructions:

1. Top and tail the plantain.
2. Peel off the plantain skin and slice into small circles on a chopping board
4. Sprinkle a pinch of salt over the plantain
5. Preheat oil in pan or deep fryer
4. Deep fry chopped plantain on medium heat on one side for 5-7minutes or until golden brown.   Flip over and repeat on other side.
6.When both sides are golden brown, Plantain is ready to be served

My Desert is:

Pancakes and ice-cream

Ingredients:

110g Plain flour (Can make 8 to 10 pancakes)
40g Sugar
2 Eggs (Medium size)
½ a pint of milk
Vanilla Essence
Golden syrup (or any syrup of your choice)
Vegetable oil
Ice-cream (any flavour)

Cooking Instructions:

1. Mix the flour and the sugar together in a bowl, making a well in the middle
2. Crack and whisk eggs and milk together into another bowl
3. Gradually incorporate the egg and milk mixture into the flour and sugar mixture
4. Add one teaspoon of vanilla essence into the mixture and stir
5. Brush a pan with oil and thinly pour batter in heated frying pan
6. Fry batter on both sides for two minutes until golden brown
7. Serve with Ice-cream of your choice and a drizzle of syrup

Kara Onuiri – Yr. 5

No Mercy

Just one stop is a tragedy,
For the Lion this is victory,
And for the young cub she is
neglected,
But that is the way of life in the
wild.

The meat is fresh but raw,
They don't care just as long as
they eat,
I stand with amazement scared
to move,
If I move I will lose my life for
good.

The cub watches her heroine being destroyed,
From now on she's alone,
She knows that and the beasts know that,
Even with the herd close by she feels alone,
She goes back to try and help.

The monster is cruising towards the cub,
Does she run or sprint,
Either way they will show no mercy,
I don't care about the beasts,
If I die, I will die with my heroine close by.

Lynda Mandu – Yr. 10

Food and Senses

I walked pass my bakery, it smelt so good,
It was like I was in heaven,
It couldn't be true,
There were so many cakes beckoning me in,
The cakes were looking at me, trying to grin.

Coke and vanilla, it's my favorite combination,
I hate to break it but it's from my nation,
It's such a sweet sensation,
As kids plunge their faces on the glass and stare,
I sit back and sulk and glare,
As I try to run away, I make a quick dash,
And before my eyes the cakes are gone in a flash.

Hannah Rawlinson – Yr. 7

Hot and Spicy

H is for how hungry you get while waiting for it to be cooked.
O is for the oooo you get when you walk in with it smelling so good.
T is for the taste you get out of it.

A is for the ahhhh you get once everyone has eaten it.
N is for the no desert wanted after it is eaten.
D is for the dessert no one ate.

S is for the slobs who stayed over.
P is for the please you get when you have to make the tea.
I is for the ice tea in the morning.
C is for the cake everyone wanted in the morning.
Y is for the yummyness in your tummy.

Chilli Paneer

- Paneer is an Indian cottage cheese to make paneer you will need:

Ingredients for Paneer:

- 6 cups of milk.
- ¼ of a cup of lemon juice. (Preferably Fresh)
- ½ a cup of water.

Method for Paneer:

- Boil the milk on medium heat and stir milk occasionally.
- Once the milk has boiled, slowly pour in lemon juice bit by bit.
- Drain out the water by using a strainer and a cheese cloth or any other thin cloth (a tea towel will do).
- Put the strainer with the towel and paneer into the sink and pour cold water onto it. this is so there is no lemon juice taste.
- Push   the paneer (in the cloth) with your hands, to try and get as much water out as possible.

- Take a pinch of paneer and try and make a smooth ball. if it does not turn into a ball then put the paneer under something heavy for about an hour. (Instead of making paneer you can buy paneer from any supermarket.)

Ingredients for Chilli Paneer:

- 1 green pepper
- 1 red pepper
- 1 red onion
- 1 white onion
- A bunch of spring onions
- 1 lemon
- Blue dragon-Thai sweet chilli sauce
- Amoy light soy sauce
- Tomato Ketchup
- Few sprigs of coriander (Fresh if possible)
- Wok / shallow pan

Preparation for Chilli Paneer:

- Chop the paneer into cubes
- Slice pepper and onions
- Wash thoroughly and chop spring onions into half horizontally (separating green shoots from white ends)
- Chop green part of spring onions in to 1cm parts.
- Chop a lemon in half and cut off a thin slice .
- (If Coriander not fresh then move on) Wash Fresh coriander thoroughly and chop finely

Method for Chilli paneer:

- Put a table spoon of oil in to a wok and heat. Make sure the oil is sizzling hot.
- Put the cubed paneer in the hot oil and every so often move it around. Leave it until slightly golden.
- Drain and leave on a paper towel to get rid of excess oil.
- Put the slices of pepper and onions into a wok and leave until cooked.
- Put the paneer back into a wok and stir all the vegetables and paneer together.
- Put half of the Thai sweet chilli

- Put between six to eight table spoons of Amoy light soy sauce.
- Add two tea spoons or one table spoon of tomato ketchup.
- Stir the sauces, vegetables and paneer together so the sauces can be absorbed by the paneer and vegetables.
- Once the sauce has thickened, turn off the heat and sprinkle the left over green spring onion and the coriander. Also put the slice of lemon on top.
- Serve hot!

Sonya Kerai – Yr.10

Amy's Delights

Amy's Café Poem

The booming, bashing of the kitchen banging.
The rumbling of the tummies,
And babies crying for their dummies.
Waiting for their mouth-watering food
And the ding of the waitress bell.
The ear-piercing squeals of the mothers.
As the food comes the little children scream yummy,
yummy in my tummy.
Babies knocking the flowers over the window sill,
And fathers moaning about paying the bill.

My Food Story

One day, in cold England, there lived a lady called Grace that loved to cook and
was very good at it. She was making something very simple- strawberries
dipped in chocolate. She was doing this to give to her friends when they came
round. She thought that they would like it because they were all very anxious
about their weight and ran every morning. When they came, they all told
Grace how delicious all the food was and how they were being so naughty by
eating so much. They had finished all the healthy food and all that was left was
the strawberries in chocolate. They all thought that they should just eat the
strawberries and leave the chocolate- so that was what they did.
When they had all gone home and Grace had gone on a run, the chocolate
sighed and said "I am so sad, people never get to eat me and when they do
they say it was naughty of them. It is so unfair when they eat grapes, they are
all so proud of themselves. I think I am going to run away." So that is what he
did. He never came back and now everybody really misses chocolate.
P.S: Chocolate has coco
beans in which are healthy.
Tell everybody especially
your parents.

Amy's Fruit Cocktail

Ingredients:

One third of raspberry and
blackberry drink
1 tea spoon of vanilla ice
cream
4 cubes of ice
100ml Fizzy orange
100ml Orange juice
One straw
One paper umbrella

Recipe:

Pour the orange juice into a
glass.
Pour the fizzy orange in.
Pour the raspberry and
blackberry juice in
Melt ice cream and put it in.
Put the ice in.
Finally put a straw and
umbrella in.

My recipe is Amy's Amazing fruit cocktail.
My cocktail is based in the Summer time because it cools you down.
It is from Spain because it is hot there. It is special to me because it is my
favourite drink and my whole family like to drink it in the summer, in the
garden.

Amy Grossmith-Dwek – Yr.7

Bhel Puri

Bhel puri was created by a Gujarati migrant to Mumbai.   Its main ingredients are puffed rice and sev, thin noodles which are made from chickpea flour and fried.   It is then mixed with boiled potatoes, chickpeas onions, and a tangy spice called Chaat. It is usually accompanied with either tangy, sweet chutney made from tamarind or green spicy chutney made from coriander leaves and green chillies.   Sold by street vendors to the passing public it is well on the way of becoming a favourite snack with the residents of Mumbai as well as tourists. Personally I love the taste of Bhel puri with green spicy chutney.   I have my own variation of the recipe.   This will make roughly two portions. My problem is that I never measure the ingredients and rely on sight to know when I have the recipe just right.

Ingredients:

2 medium sized potatoes.   Diced, boiled and drained.
1can of chick peas, drained.
Savoury puffed rice and thin gram flour noodles fried.   Also known as sev and can be bought ready made.
Handful of peanuts
Green coriander to garnish.
FOR THE LIQUID/CHUTNEY
Fresh finely chopped coriander
Fresh mint finely chopped
1 tablespoon whole cumin seeds crushed.
Lemon juice, Black salt to taste.
Water.
Place water in a pot and add all the ingredients to it and let it sit for half an hour.   Check for taste and adjust whatever ingredient is required and then strain the liquid and leave to one side.   If you wish for a thicker chutney you may add more coriander, chillies or mint.

To Eat:

Mix the potatoes with some of the chick peas in a plate.
Layer the puffed rice and sev on top.
Garnish with green coriander and peanuts.
Pour as much or as little of the liquid or chutney as required and savour to your heart's content.

A life in song

Samar was having a hard time at work. He was finding it harder to concentrate and it was becoming more and more tiresome to deal with people as they came in with one thing or another. On top of that he hadn't been able to pull Sanya out of the mood she was feeling no matter what he did and it was bugging the hell out of him. He knew he was at fault somehow but until she told him he would not have a clue. All he could make out was that it was connected to the recent Holi celebrations. There was a rap at the door and he sighed in frustration.

"Come in!" He called out irritably and Hayat sauntered in and placed the four reports he had given her this afternoon, on his desk.

"Here are the reports you asked for and my recommendations." She said removing the earphone from her ear, placing the wire in her trouser pocket and looking at his disgruntled features she smiled. There was a devil-may-care attitude about her coupled with a mischievous glint in her eye. She knew that he would tear a strip off her but she could not stop herself.
"Who rattled your chain?" She asked. Samar's face darkened.
"What?" She saw the anger, but it didn't stop her. She put her hands up in mock surrender.
"Hey. I just asked a question. You have a face like someone has promised you heaven but gave you the shitty side of earth instead." He took a deep breath ready to blast her, but there was a something in her eyes and the way she looked at him, teasing him to come out of his bad mood that made him stop and think and he found himself answering her.
"I am having a few issues." Hayat pulled up a chair and sat down expectantly waiting to hear more. He shook his head at her action and allowed the briefest of smiles and then put up a barrier again "They are my personal issues and that is all I am going to say."
"Tease!" She said and stood up. "Well whatever it is you'd better sort it out. You're a right grump. What's up? Are you in the dog house?" Samar thought to rebuke her but decided against it. He had been a nightmare to his staff today.
"It is 5pm on a Friday. Shouldn't you be going home now?"
"Ah yes, home." She said rather shamefacedly and looked down briefly. He looked bemused. That face had to be an act. He had seen it in Manish, his brother, when he was in teasing mode or needed something. She looked at him and with a cheeky smile and asked.

"Um. I don't have enough money for the bus home. Could you lend me some money until Monday?"

"How is it that you are short of cash? Go along to the office and ask to borrow some money from petty cash instead." That smile again.

"There is nobody in the office. I have a lavish lifestyle to lead. You know partying, drinking, gambling. And the weekend is my own and it is not complete until I have visited Jignesh Bhai's food stall and had some bhel puri." Samar reached into his pocket and pulled out his wallet. He handed over a note. Hayat took it, placed it in her own wallet and smiled at him.

"Cheers." She quipped and sauntered out of the office leaving Samaar standing there. She turned back. "You know. A lot of misunderstandings happen when people don't talk to each other. You only have one life in this world. It is too short to be angry with each other and looking back with regrets. Whatever it is that is troubling you, it is up to you to find the solution. For all our sakes." She smiled. "You are too stuffy. You should lose yourself in music." And with that she turned and left.

"Did that really happen?" He mused. He could never figure her out. She was an excellent worker, had weird practices, but could always be found working away while connected to her ipod. No one had a bad word to say against her and in the time since she had joined the company she had proved invaluable. He likened her manner to that of a happy-go-lucky pizza delivery boy. With not a care in the world working away at his own pace, whistling, singing and ignoring everything and everyone else.

Manish arrived at the door half an hour later.

"Bhai? Are you ready to leave?" Samar nodded and proceeded to pack away his laptop and files. He picked up his car keys and heard something drop from the table. He picked it up. It was Hayat's ipod. He looked down and smiled and then looked at Manish

"Hayat has left her ipod. It is her life and she will miss it. We should call her and return it. Can you get her number from the personnel files and we will call her as we leave and drop it off to her.

"Yes. Bhai." Said Manish and pulled out Hayat's file and noted her number. On the way to the car he dialled her number. After three rings she picked up.

"Hello?"

"Hayat? It's Manish. You have left your iPod here and Samar Bhai said that we should drop it off to you."

"No. No. Don't worry. I'll pick it up on Monday. It has got some good songs on it. Tell your Samar Bhai to listen to some of the songs. He might just loosen up."

The stuffed shirt!" She laughed. "Have a good weekend. I shall see you on Monday."

The Friday evening traffic was as busy as they had anticipated and both boys resigned themselves to sit it out as they made their journey home. Manish was curious about the contents of the ipod. He waved it at Samar.

"Bhai? Can I put this on?" Samar looked and nodded. Normally he would have had the radio on so he was not too bothered. Manish connected up the device and went through the playlist. "So many songs." He said. "She has got Bruno Mars, Soul, Motown, Enrique, Some Indian songs, Linkin Park and All American Rejects. What do you want to listen to?"

"Just put it on." Samar replied, slowing the car as the anticipated traffic hit. They sat listening to the first song and smiled.

"Bhai." Manish faced Samar. "Do you remember when we were younger we used to sit and listen to music all weekend long?" Samar chuckled.

"I remember. And Meena used to want to sit with us and drive us mad with her chatter. Do you remember the time when we locked her in the bathroom and went out to play cricket?" Manish sat back in his seat and laughed out loud.

"How could I forget? When we came back in she was in a right state. She had screamed so much. I was so scared seeing her all angry and crying like that. I thought that we were done for." Kaki(Aunty) was so mad. Samar laughed and shook his head.

"Hope this traffic lets up. I am dying to get home." Manish looked at him quizzically.

"Have you sorted things out with Bhabi then?" Samar shook his head.

"Not yet. But I intend to find out what exactly is wrong. I can't be doing with this silent treatment and hiding anymore."

"Bhai. There is no need to hide yourself away. You are a grown up now." Manish joked. Samar shook his head. There was no indication that the cars would start moving any time soon. He reached for the ipod and chose a song at random. As luck would have it, it was Grenade by Bruno Mars.

As the words of the song's chorus rang out both reflected on the events of their domestic life.

"catch a grenade for ya ......
I'd do anything for ya ....
I would die for you baby ....
You won't do the same ....

They looked at each other with unease and then with a realisation. The lyrics were an exact mirror for each boy. Samar had Sanya's adulation where she had loved him from day one and would do anything for his happiness.

Manish was prepared to give Aarti the world and yet she kept him further and further away from her. He made every effort to make sure that she was comfortable but she brushed aside his declarations of love and continued to chase for materialistic things.

Two pairs of eyes looked at each other. One set acknowledging the hurt and pain already caused and the relief at being given a chance and the other filled with the confusion and pain caused by rejection.

"We have a lot of work to do one way or another." Noted Samar. Manish sighed.

"Sometimes it feels like Aarti does not care for me. I have known since the day we were married that she always wanted the materialistic things and that is the reason why she married me. But I always hoped that cupid's arrow will hit her the same way it hit you. Maybe something drastic needs to be done."

"Maybe? If she realises that she can no longer take you for granted she may change."

"What you mean like treat them mean to keep them keen," Manish laughed.

"No. You have got to make Aarti realise your worth. The same way that Sanya made me realise what she is worth to me." He said wistfully. "And now she is upset with me and I do not know why." Samar saw that the traffic was moving and manoeuvred the car through the throng of vehicles. By the time they hit the intersection the road was clear and they cruised along the motorway. "What else does she have? This maestro of the ipod?" He asked. Manish looked at the ipod and chose the Pet Shop Boys song "Always on my mind."

Samar's mind wandered as he listened to the words of the song. Realising that every word rang true to the way he had treated Sanya in the past and the wish to be given another chance. He felt ashamed at the way he had treated her and his mind replayed all those horrible scenes one after the other. Far too many to think about. He shook his head as if to clear away the cobwebs.

"Are you alright Bhai?" asked Manish. Samar nodded.

"Choose the next song?" Manish leaned forward and set the ipod on to shuffle. Giving them a whole catalogue of songs. They listened in silence to the songs finding that the day's tensions were beginning to ease away.

They weren't far from home when the final song came on. Lobo's "I'd love you to want me." They smiled as the song started and Manish put the volume up and sat back in the seat. As the song continued images flashed through Samar's mind. He vaguely remembered dancing on holi. Something he never did. He remembered wanting to colour Sanya and wish her a happy holi but something always stopped him. He wound down the window and took a deep breath, checked the traffic which was sparse and continued driving. His mind thought about holi again. This time he was in the house with Sanya and he was throwing colour at her, chasing her through the house and then ending up in the bedroom. As a third person he watched as he raced towards her, crash straight into her and ended up on the bed itself. Then? Nothing. His brow furrowed. What had gone on? Then the thought hit him. "Was the reason for Sanya's tears, her anger and distance down to something he had done? They had ended up on the bed. Could he have crossed that last barrier with her? Had she been unwilling?" The last question shocked and repulsed him.

He slammed on the brakes. Causing the car to turn 180 degrees facing the oncoming traffic and leave the road, ending up on the grassy verge. Manish felt his head spin for a moment and fearfully he looked over at his brother. Samar sat stock still, breathing deeply staring straight ahead. Manish became concerned. Samar looked deathly pale, sweaty and he was shaking uncontrollably.

"Bhai? What happened?" No answer. He put his hand out and shook Samar by the arm. "Bhai? Speak to me. What's wrong?" Samar turned and looked at him with unseeing eyes. With shaking hands he released himself from his seatbelt and got out of the car. Reaching the grass verge he sank to his knees and was sick. Manish feared for Samar. His brother had never been like this before. He picked up a water bottle, got out of the car and went to him. He squatted next to him and tried to coax an answer out of him. After a while Samar stopped shaking.

"Bhai?" Concern was etched on Manish's face. "What's wrong?" Samar took the water bottle and sipped a little before spilling the contents into his hands and splashed his face. He placed his hand on Manish's shoulder, reassuring him that he was fine.

"I am ok." He finally said. "I just felt sick." Manish looked on.

"Are you alright now? Do you want me to drive the rest of the way?" Samar nodded and they made their way back to the car. Manish got into the driver's seat, shot one final look at Samar belting himself in. Samar looked at Manish.

"I'll be fine. Please. Start driving." Manish turned the car the right way and headed for home as quickly as possible.

Samar had calmed down considerably by the time they pulled up at the house.

"Manish? I'd be grateful if you didn't mention anything at home."

"But Bhai?"

"Whatever it was has passed." He looked at the house. "Now you and I have got a lot of things we need to sort out with our wives. Let us use this weekend to sort these things out."

"As long as you're sure that you're fine?" Samar smiled.

"All I need is to get in. Get a glimpse of Sanya's face, a cup of tea and a change of clothing. I am fine." He reassured Manish again and prayed that he would get some answers tonight and a chance to put things right.

After bidding everyone a greeting Samar searched for Sanya and found her on the terrace. Without a word he grabbed her hand and took her to the bedroom. Once inside he broke the habit of a lifetime and locked the door. Sanya looked at him indifferently.

"Do you want something?" She asked.

"Some answers would be nice." She looked at him puzzled. He looked back at her. Should he play nice and coax the events of holi out of her. No. If anything she will not tell him. She will play it down and sacrifice her feelings for his wellbeing. For the moment he hardened his heart and made believe that he was back in those early dark days when he had abused her, belittled her and downright treated her badly. He advanced on her and stared.

"I want to know exactly what happened here on holi." He said in a low voice. Sanya sensed his anger and shrank back. "Tell me!" he shouted. She jumped. He grabbed her by the shoulders and shook her. Tears welled in her eyes. She had been promised the world and then had it cruelly taken away from her in the spate of a day. And now this was adding salt to an open wound. She had lost him forever. With nothing further to lose began.

"On holi you kept looking at me and wanting to speak to me but we kept getting disturbed. Then aunty gave me some juice and when I bumped into you I gave it to you. It the time I did not know that it had been laced with drugs. Afterwards you danced and then we had a photograph taken and then you kept saying that you were hungry so we went into the house to get you something to eat."

"And then?" There was a tenderness in his voice but Sanya failed to hear it.

"We stood in front of the temple. You wouldn't let me cover my head with the sari.. You then coloured me and wished me happy holi and asked me if I was going to colour and wish you too. So I did and then I ran away from you." The image of him running after her and throwing colour at her flashed through his mind. As she spoke all the images came clearly to him and finally the veil of uncertainty lifted. Inwardly he heaved a sigh of relief. What he had feared was baseless. But she was still upset with him.

"Is that the reason why you were upset with me?" he asked and there was no way that she could ignore the change in his tone.

"I was given a chance to touch the sky." She replied. "By nightfall you had removed my wings. I was shattered that you did not remember." He held her hands in his.

"Sanya I am sorry that I did not remember. But slowly things are coming back to me and until they do you will have to tell me exactly what went on in here." Sanya gulped.

Meanwhile in his room Manish was waiting. He paced the room up and down and thought of what he should say. He had already been over and over the words he had said to her when he found out all she had done and the deceit to marry him. He was in these same thoughts when Aarti walked in the room. Her phone glued to her ear, talking away nineteen to the dozen. As soon as she saw him she stopped.

"OK Mummy. Thanks for that. I have to go. Talk to you later. Bye." She cut the call and came to him. "Manishji? When did you come home? I didn't see you." Manish looked at her and thought back to her phone call.

"Why is it that everytime she talks to her mother, something goes wrong here." He thought to himself.

"I looked for you." He found himself replying. "But you were nowhere in the house."

"I was in the kitchen." She said. "And I did not hear the door."

"I came into the kitchen but you weren't there." He scanned her features.

"No," she dismissed him. "I meant to say that I was on the terrace."

"Liar!" He thought to himself but continued in an even tone. "I went to the terrace. I didn't see you." He had seen her. She had not been on the terrace. He had spotted her in the garden.

"No. What I meant to say was that I was in the garden."

"Bingo." He thought.

"Who were you on the phone to?"

"The phone? It was just a friend." He looked sternly at her and finally the penny dropped for her. She was lying to him and she looked down shamefaced. "Actually, I was talking to my mother." Manish sighed in frustration.

"You could have told me sooner. Come and sit with me a while." And he grabbed her hand and pulled her towards him. She tried to free herself and moved away from him.

"Manishji. What are you doing?" She looked towards the door. "Somebody may see."

"So what if someone sees." He jerked her back towards him. "I am your husband. Don't you wish to spend some time with me?" She was still trying to squirm out of his grip.

"Manishji. Please. I have so much work to do. If I don't go now kakiji will scold me." A spark of anger flared in him.

"What work, Aarti? You yourself said that you were in the garden earlier on when everyone else was working. What is there to do now? As far as I know everything has been done." He looked into her eyes.

"I asked you this question once before Aarti and now I am asking it again. Have you ever loved me?" Aarti looked at him opening and shutting her mouth. As if trying to find the right words to say. She saw a change come over Manish. He looked disappointed. Defeated even. "Aarti, your silence speaks volumes to me. I wanted to give you the best of everything. But you just threw it back at me. Why? What advice is it that you are getting from your mother that makes you want to run away from me?"

"Manishji. It is nothing like that. Mummy just tells me little bits of gossip."

"It is everything like that," he said. "Everytime I get that little bit closer to you, you run away. Aarti. I am not going to be patient forever. I have made a decision. As of now I will not chase you, cajole you, humour you or place any demands on you. When you do decide that you want this relationship then you will have to come to me. I am fed up of doing the running round anymore." He picked up his phone and left the room, making a phone call to discontinue Aarti's contract on her phone. He felt bad but it had to be done. If she rejected him, she rejected all that he could give her. It would start with the phone. She would have to learn to live without speaking to that jealous, irritating woman who constantly poured poison into her ears and created misunderstandings.

The weekend passed by with a few changes. Samar and Sanya were more comfortable in each other's company and even spent one day out of the family house finally doing things a normal married couple do. Manish became more aloof with Aarti and the initial indications were positive. Aarti, did not like being ignored and felt uncomfortable. No longer able to run to her mother for ideas to cause more mayhem, she was making more of an effort with Manish. True she had screamed at him when she found out about the phone, but she had eventually calmed down. He knew that he still had a way to go and was happy to wait. Things would go finally his way in the end. The ipod itself went back and forth between both boys and they enjoyed listening intently to the songs and realised the there was a truth in what Hayat had said.

It was a different Samar who turned up for work on Monday morning. He was still the efficient business man but he conducted himself better. With Manish by his side they made a formidable team and they dealt with the day's work with renewed vigour. It was past lunch when they both sat down.

"That was a good batch of meetings this morning, Bhai. We have a number of projects which are taking off. Dad will be proud."

"He always is. Are things any better between you and Aarti? Sorry I should have asked you earlier."

"Don't worry. You were too busy with Bhabi to take any notice of me." He said good naturedly. "But it's ok. I have laid a few ground rules and if Aarti wants to be with me then she has to make the first move." Samar raised his eyebrows.

"Do you think it will work?"

"I don't know Bhai. But I do know that there is scope for Aarti to accept me. And I am prepared to see where that will take me."

"Hope it works out the way you have planned." He reached for his bag and picked it up. Hayat's ipod dropped out. He picked it up and turned it over in his hand. "We should give this back. He picked up his phone and dialled through to his secretary. "Hello, Indu. Can you ask Hayat to come to my office please? Thank you." He replaced the receiver and turned to Manish. "She was right about the songs, helping to resolve things."

"And made you less of a stuffy shirt." Manish laughed. The phone rang and Samar hit the speaker button. It was Indu.

"Sir. Personnel say that she did not come in today." Samar looked at Manish. "Did she call in?" He asked.

"No Sir."

"OK. Thanks." He hit the disconnect button. "That's not like her. Perhaps we ought to drop off the ipod back to her. She is that lost without it that she has not turned up today. Although I think I might have to fight her for it." Samar cracked a joke and Manish looked at him dumbfounded. His bhai was definitely not a stuffed shirt now.

As evening fell both boys packed up their belongings and headed for the car. They stopped off at personnel to get Hayat's address. Manish gave directions as Samar drove. On the way there Samar spied a street vendor. Jignesh's Paani and Bhel Puri. Samar remembered Hayat enthusing about the food and stopped the car. Manish looked at him.

"What are we doing?" Samar smiled ruefully.

"Hayat mentioned that this guy does the best bhel puri this side of Mumbai. We are here. Why not give it a try? See if it is just as good as she raved about?" They walked towards the humble cart with hand painted signs advertising its wares. The vendor was all too pleased with his passing trade and happily offered up two portions of bhel puri to them. Manish licked his fingers.

"Bhai. Hayat was not wrong. This is really good." The vendor's ears picked up. "Hayatji told you about me?" He smiled. "She is my biggest champion. She tells everyone about my stall. I am very happy she mentions me." They chatted with the vendor for a while and then went on their way. After half an hour they pulled up outside the address listed. They knocked on the door and waited as they heard shuffling and then the door was opened by a silver haired, elderly man who blinked up at them.

"Hello." Samar greeted him. "We would like to meet with Hayat."

"Hayat?" The old man repeated and then showed them into the house. "Sit, sit." He ushered them into the small sitting room and into two well-worn seats and went off muttering something. He then came back with a young lad. "This is my son." He said and sat down. "What can we do for you?" Manish took out the ipod from his pocket.

"We have come to return something of Hayat's. She left it at work." He held it out to the young lad, who made no effort to take it from him but instead looked at the old man. Manish drew back his hand, puzzled.

"We missed Hayat at work today. It's very unlike her. Is she your granddaughter? Can we see her for a few minutes?" Samar asked. The old man looked at the young man sat by his side and then at them. He shook his head. "Beta. Hayat is not my granddaughter." He said eventually. "She is my wife."

The shock showed on both boys' faces. They were finding it hard to comprehend that someone as carefree as Hayat could be married and that too to a man old enough to be her grandfather.

"Your wife!" They chorused together and then remembered their manners and looked on in confusion. The old man showed no emotion.

"You are surprised." He said. "Five years ago I married Hayat as part of a trade-off. Her brother had eloped with my youngest granddaughter. As is the custom in our village I approached the tribal elders for justice. They passed judgement and we were married." Samar and Manish were horrified.

"And you agreed to it?" Samar didn't know who he was more disgusted with. At the old man for even considering the alliance or the judgment of the village elders who had passed judgement on an innocent. Either way what type of life had been handed to Hayat? Slowly he was beginning to feel the anger rise in him. The old man shrugged.

"I had lost my wife six months earlier. I needed someone to look after me in my old age. This was an answer to my problem."

"Is she here?" Samar asked keeping his voice as level as possible.

"Yes we would like to meet with her." The old man shook his head.

"Not possible." He said and stood up. "I think perhaps you had better leave."

"But we would like to meet Hayat before we leave." Insisted Samar, stripping aside any respect he held for the individual who stood before him. The old man sighed and looked at the shelf above the fireplace.

"Hayat went out on Friday night. She never came home. She was listening to her music on her phone and did not hear the car coming up behind her. Hayat is no more."

The impact of those words hit both of them much harder than they thought. They left the house in silence and made their way home. Stopping the car outside MM they sat. Finally Manish spoke.

"Bhai. I don't know what to say. I don't know how to feel. What kind of life did she have?" Tears glistened in his eyes. Samar shook his head.

"Whatever she did have, she dealt with it in the only way she knew how." He turned the iPod round in his hand and sighed. "In all the time that she worked with us I cannot recall one day when she was down. I never heard one word of complaint from her and I don't think anyone else did either. Can't believe how some parents are willing to bargain with their daughters. But do you know what has bothered me the most?" Manish looked at him. "I saw sadness in that house. But not at her passing. I saw no signs of mourning. They will not miss her for who she was."

"Should we do something?"

"Perhaps."

"Maybe we could do something to remember her by? We could make Bhel puri for all our staff and spend some time listening to her music." Samar nodded giving it serious thought.

Hayat had, had such a profound effect on both boys in the shortest of times. She had helped them overcome the hurdles in their relationships to provide them with a better understanding. Ironically, the translation of her name meant life. Her's was cut short but she breathed new life into others wherever she had been. And as things worked out they would never forget her. Whenever they ate Bhel puri the looked to the horizon and smile inwardly.

Xarina (Zahidah Akhtar), Staff

Recipe for a Bulgarian yogurt and cucumber starter
"TARATOR"

This is a nice and easy cold starter to make, ideal for those hot summer days. In the past, it would be served chilled to farm workers for lunch and was usually followed by a good, hearty main meal.

Products (serves 6):

- 1 cucumber,
- 1 ½ pots of plain yogurt
- Dill
- 2-3 cloves of garlic
- 2 tbs olive oil
- 1ts salt

Preparation:

Dice the cucumber 1cm cubes and put in a pot. Add the finely chopped garlic and dill. Season with salt. Dilute the yogurt with some water. You could make the yogurt as thick as you like it. I usually dilute it in the ratio of 1:1 ½ yogurt to water. Pour in the pot. Add the oil and stir well. Chill in the fridge for about half an hour. Enjoy!
A variation of this Tarator is replacing the yogurt with some water and some vinegar to taste.

Annie Lalova - Staff

Banana Frozen Yoghurt

Ingredients:

- 2 bananas
- 300g natural stir yoghurt
- 100ml semi-skimmed milk
- 3 table spoons granulated sugar
1 teaspoon lemon juice

Method:

1. Heat the milk with a microwave oven for one minute and dissolve the sugar.
2. Peel the Banana and add the lemon juice and smash it until it becomes a puree using the back of a fork.
3. Blend the milk and yoghurt with the banana. Pour it in the tray and freeze.
4. Stir it with a fork or a spoon if it is about to harden. Repeat this several times.

Yuri Nabesawa – Yr. 2

Summer Pudding

This is a pleasant, tasty and easy pudding to prepare.

Ingredients:

White bread (preferably 1-2 days old), sliced and crusts removed.
2 tablespoons of water
5 ozs sugar
1lb of mixed summer fruits (blackcurrants, strawberries, raspberries, redcurrants, blackberries etc)- These can be fresh or frozen
A round pyrex bowl smeared on the inside with butter or sunflower spread (this allows easy removal of the pudding from the dish)
These ingredients can be increased if necessary depending on how many you are catering for.

Method:

Add the water and sugar to a pan and slowly bring to the boil
Add the fruit to the pan and bring back to the boil
Turn the heat down and allow the fruit to simmer for 15-20 minutes
Meanwhile prepare the bowl and line it with the sliced decrusted bread
When the fruit is soft but still retains its shape, use a strainer spoon to transfer the fruit to the lined dish
Cover the fruit with another slice of bread and seal the pudding by placing a saucer over the top with a weight on it to hold the top down while it cools
Pour the juice from the pan into a container to be used when serving the pudding
When the pudding has cooled sufficiently, place it in the refrigerator overnight
Just before serving, ease the pudding out of the bowl and invert it onto a serving dish
Cover it with the juice
Decorate it with fresh fruit and serve it with cream or crème fraiche

Mrs Smith – Staff

Grace's Meringue Mess Poem

It's weird,
It's wonderful,
It's bright,
Its light,
She brings everyone,
Sheer delight.

Crunchy and soft,
All mixed together,
You can eat it,
Whatever the weather.

Grace's Meringue Mess

My recipe is meringue mess.

This recipe is special to me because I created it myself and it is great fun to make and I love to make a mess.

This recipe is for the season summer

Ingredients:

Meringue
Strawberries
Raspberries
Bananas
Whip cream
Strawberry sauce
Raspberry sauce.

Method:

1: Break up your meringue into a bowl.
2: Add your whip cream.
3: Add your strawberries, raspberries and bananas.
4: Mix in your strawberry sauce and raspberry sauce.
Now get ready to eat messy.

Grace Kindall - Yr.7

Fruitilicious Milkshake

Ingredients

10 Blueberries
10 Raspberries
1 chopped Banana
200ml of milk
3 Scoops of vanilla ice cream
1 Blender

Recipe

1: Put the 200ml of milk into the blender.
2: Put the 2 scoops of ice cream in there.
3: Put all the fruits into the blender.
4: Blend all the mixture tighter for about 1 minuet, until the mixture is a liquid form.
5: Put in a glass and add the final blob of ice cream on the top.

Where this recipe comes from?

This recipe comes from Grandma, when she was trying to get me to eat fruit as a young child. I still use the recipe today.

Why this is important to me?

This recipe is important to me because it reminds me of the times with my Grandma.

What season it relates to?

This recipe relates to the season summer because of the fruit and ice cream used in the recipe.

Rachel Price – Yr.7

Fruit Smoothies

Ingredients:

- 1 Banana
- 60g (2oz) Strawberries
- 2 Peaches
- 110g (4oz) vanilla yoghurt
110ml (4 fl.oz) orange juice

Recipe:

1. Cut a few slices from the banana and strawberries and put the rest into a blender.
2. Peel the peaches and put the flesh into the blender.
3. Add the yoghurt and orange juice to the fruit and whizz until smooth.
4. Push the left over strawberry and banana slices onto straws and serve.

Kiani Patel – Yr.2

Caramel Banana Cake

Ingredients - For Cake

- Butter 120g
- Caster Sugar 100g
- 3 eggs
- Self-raising flour100g
- Rum1 table spoon
- 2 bananas

For Caramel Sauce

- Caster Sugar 80g
- Water 2 teaspoon
- Hot Water 2 teaspoon

You need

- 18cm rounding baking tin (not loose base)
- Greaseproof paper
- A bowl
- Hand mixer
- Sifter
- Scale
- Spatula

Introduction:

- Take out the eggs and butter from fridge 30 minutes ago.
- Sift the self-raising flour.
- Cut the greaseproof paper round.
- Spread the shortening around the baking tin.
- Put the greaseproof paper inside the baking tin.

Preparation Method:

1 Put caster sugar (80g) and water into the small pan. Heat the pan until the colour changes into brown. Do not burn. After the colour changes, take off the pan from heat and put hot water in it. Then put them into baking tin.

2. Cut the bananas into 7~8mm. Place them in the baking tin.Preheat the oven to 165.

3. Cream the butter in the bowl. Then add the caster sugar in three times. Rub it until pale and fluffy.

4. Beat in the eggs. Then add them in above 3 in 5~6times and mix them. Make it creamy. Add rum and mix them again.

5.Change the handmixer into spatula and add self-raising flour into the bowl. Fold it until no powder is seen.

6. Turn the mixture into baking tin and make their surface smooth. Put them into the oven. Bake it for 35 minutes until a skewer comes out clean. Remove from the oven and turn over the tin and take out the cake. Then take off the greaseproof paper.

Why it is my favourite:

- Because I like bananas and caramel.
- My sister was making this cake when she was in year 5 and I want to make and eat them again.

Momoko Yamane – Yr. 5

Delicious Magic Lemon Pudding

Sponge

What you will need:

Sponge

- 100g Flour
- 100g Butter
- 100g Sugar
- 2 eggs
- Grated rind of 1 lemon
- 1 table spoon of milk

Sauce

- 100g Sugar
- 2 table spoons corn flour
- Juice of 1 lemon

Enough boiling water to make up 300ml

What to do:

1. Grease a 1 litre oven proof dish
2. Beat all the sponge ingredients together and pour in dish
3. Combine sugar, corn flour, lemon juice and boiling water.
4. Pour on top of the mixture
5. Bake for 35 minutes and you will have yummy lemon cake with the sauce all underneath like magic!

I love this pudding!

Phoebe Brady – Yr. 5

Lemon Drizzle Cake

Lemon drizzle cake is from the Summer time. I choose the recipe because it is very yummy and I always make it for my family. It is the recipe that my great grandma used to make when I went to her house. Lemon drizzle cake is from England.

Ingredients:

- 225g unsalted butter
- 225g of caster sugar
- 4 eggs
- I lemon
- 225g of self-raising flour

For the drizzle:

Juice of one and a half lemons
85g of caster sugar

Method:

Heat the oven at 180c.
Beat together the butter and the caster sugar. Do this until pale and creamy.
Add the eggs
Next sieve the flour.
Grate the zest of the lemon and add it.
Mix
Line the tin with greaseproof paper and add the mixture.
Leave it in the oven for 40-45 mins
To check if it is done insert a skewer into the middle of the cake, if it comes out clean it is done if not leave it longer.
Mix together the juice of one and a half lemons and 85g of caster sugar to make the drizzle.
Lastly add the drizzle and leave to cool.
Eat it!!!!!

Amy Grossmith-Dwek – Yr.7

Lemon Treats

How to Make Homemade Lemonade:

Ingredients:

* 2 lemons
* Sugar (6-8 table spoons depending on your taste)
* Water (still or sparkling)
* Ice
* ½ a lime

To make homemade lemonade, start by pouring the sugar into a mug and adding about ¼ of a cup of boiling hot water (to dissolve the sugar). Then juice the lemons and ½ a lime. Pour the lemon and lime juice in to a glass, then add in the dissolved sugar and mix for about 1 minute. Next stir in the water and ice. Once you have made the lemonade you can add in some slices of lemons and limes for decoration.

Why I like it:

This recipe for homemade lemonade is the best as it so simple and most the ingredients can be found in the kitchen so you can make it whenever you want without having to worry about not having the right ingredients. The recipe is also very flexible and can be changed exactly to your tastes, by adding more or less sugar, depending on how much of a sweet tooth you have.
Once you have tried this homemade lemonade you will never want anything else. Everyone you know will forever be asking you to make more as it tastes so amazing.

Preamble:

I came across this recipe when I was on holiday. I was sitting on the beach in the hot summer sun, when my mum came over to me with a glass of lemonade. After one sip of this lemonade I straight away knew it was the best lemonade I had ever tasted.

Lauren Perkins – Yr. 9

Lemon Sorbet

Oh lemon sorbet!
How much I love devouring you
On a hot summers day.
The way you taste
Has a pleasant place
On my sugar-loving,
Luscious lips...

Yummy and lovely,
The lemon sorbet I made,
Sticky and messy!
The lemon sorbet I made.

Trinity Perkins – Yr.7

How to Make the Lemon Sorbet

Ingredients you will need:

3 lemons (cold)
1 cup of sugar
2 teaspoons of golden syrup (optional)
2 ½ cups of very cold water

Method:

1. First grate the zest from one lemon and then put it aside
2. Then juice all of the lemons into a cup
3. Take out all of the pips from the juice
4. Afterwards stir the sugar, syrup and water into a mixing bowl
5. Stir until everything dissolves
6. Once everything has dissolved, stir in the lemon and zest
7. Put the mixture into an ice-cream maker or simply in the freezer.

Lemon Story

Lemon sorbet comes from the summer season, it comes in handy on a hot summer's day, it cools you down when you are hot and it is so refreshing to eat, you can even wait for it to melt and have it as chilled lemonade.

I chose the lemon sorbet because it brings back all the memories from going to the park back to sitting on the beach and scraping every single mouthful or drop you could get out of the toucan tub in Italy.

No one is sure where lemon sorbet comes from but it is said it either comes from Rome, China or the Middle East.

My experiences when eating lemon sorbet have mainly been clean but one time on a very hot summer day, I made lemon sorbet but it was after when things got sticky. It starts when my friends arrive, we planned out our day the first thing we did was go on my brand new water slide (it was so cool) then we sat down on the garden table and ate some of my delicious, refreshing sorbet, the door bell rung and it was my cheeky uncle. My friends and I didn't hear the doorbell ring and when I was just about to lick my sorbet off the cone, my uncle pushed my head down into the sorbet.   All my friends burst out laughing; that was most probably the funniest thing that has happened to me with sorbet.

Trinity Perkins – Yr. 7

Sponge Cake

Ingredients:

- 110 g butter
- 110 g caster sugar
- 2 eggs
- 110 g self-rising flour

Instructions:

1) Cream together the butter and the sugar
2) Add the eggs and flour. Stir until consistent.
3) Grease the base of a tin. Pour the mixture in and flatten with a spatula!
4) Bake for 30 minutes at gas mark 4/ 180 degrees Celsius!
5) Leave the cake to cool, then slice!

Ice cream cake

Ingredients:

- 1 litre of ice cream.
- Chocolate chips

Instructions:

1) Split the ice cream
2) Put greaseproof paper in the bottom of a tin and pour half the ice cream in.
3) Pour the chocolate chips on top and leave in the freezer for 3 hours.
4) Do the same with the other one freezing for 3 hours as well
5) Place both on top of each other and put back in the freezer for 1 hour
6) Slice the cake.

Where my cake comes from...

My cake was just an accident I had a bowl of ice-cream in front of a cupboard and the chocolate chips fell out, and then I had an IDEA!
My recipe is for spring!

Gemma Hook – Yr.7

Victoria Sponge

Her name was Victoria,
She was fluffy and soft,
Her middle so creamy,
I like her a lot,
Her top so white, so fluffy, so light,
She can't help but bring people delight.
Her last name was Sponge,
She was the undefeatable,
Better than the cheesecake,
And the treacle,
She smelt so sweet,
And looked it too,
She is the perfect dessert for you!

Mystery Mess

Dear Grandma,

How are you? I have missed you so much. Last week was Dad's Birthday. I got him a special wax for his car. Yesterday I made so many things; a meringue mess, a cheesecake and a Victoria sponge (your favorite).

I was just about to add the bananas when it all just disappeared with a puff of smoke and flash of light. I was so scared but then a note appeared and it said "if you want your mess come and follow the clues!" I was so confused but I wanted my mess, so I followed and found the clues which lead to a tree. I thought that was impossible and walked away.

Bizarrely the tree said something. I couldn't really understand what it meant but I did what it said. It had told me to go to my little brother. I went. He threw a pie in my face. I screamed but he ran away. Mum called me to the kitchen and she flung ice cream at me. I was furious and stormed to my bedroom where I found pasta all over my bed.

It was then that the TV presenter from 'Got Ya' jumped out of my cupboard and told me I was on the program and my family were pranking me. I wouldn't have minded but they had eaten my meringue mess.

Look forward to hearing your news.

Love Gracie xxx

By Grace Kindall – Yr.7

Ice Berry Treats

My Recipe for blueberry ice cream

Ingredients:

* 1 pint of small blueberries (400grams)
* ¾ cup of sugar
* ½ a lemon
* 1 large egg
* 1 cup of double cream
* ½ a cup of milk

Instructions:

To make the cream base for this ice cream: Start by whisking the egg in a mixing bowl util it is fluffy and light. Add in ½ a cup of sugar to the eggs. Keep whisking the eggs and adding the sugar a bit at a time. Once the mixture is completely blended add in the cream and milk to the mixture and continue to whisk.

To make the blueberry ice cream: Start by putting the blueberries, ¼ cup of sugar, and the lemon juice (squeeze ½ a lemon to get juice) in a mixing bowl. Cover the mixture and refrigerate for about two hours stirring every 30 minutes.

Crush the blueberries, until pureed and add them into the cream base, stir. Transfer the mixture into an ice-cream maker, following the recommended settings.

Why I like it:

I really like this recipe for blueberry ice-cream, as it is a family recipe that my sister and I love to make because little preparation is needed and it doesn't require much effort. The result of this ice-cream is fantastic. The creamy, rich flavours of the ever so sweet blueberries mixed with the cold chill of the ice cream tingling your taste buds, making you constantly want more. I find that this ice-cream tastes amazing, all year round but I personally like it most on a hot summers day, too cool me down and enjoy with friends and family, as it bring us all just that little bit closer together.

Lauren Perkins – Yr.9

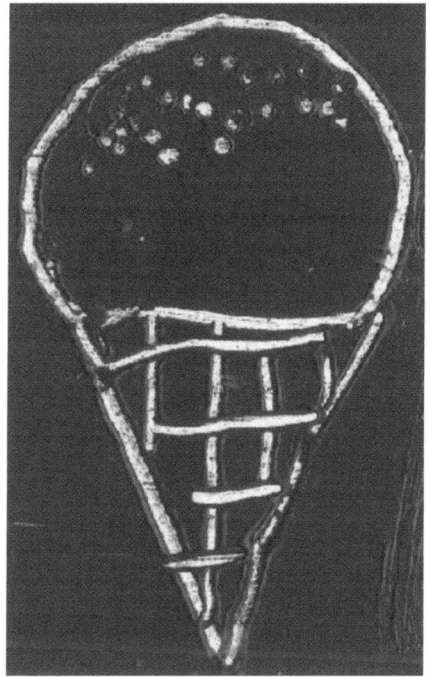

I Choose Strawberry Milkshake

Strawberry milkshake comes from the summer season; it is lovely to drink in the morning with your freshly made pancakes. It's divine when you make it with fresh strawberries and don't you just love it when you squirt the biggest amount of whipped cream on the top.

I chose strawberry milkshake because it reminds me off all my friends when we would go out to a milkshake house and have a contest of who could glug down there milkshake the fastest and whoever did wouldn't have to pay for their shake.

My experiences when drinking strawberry milkshake have always been delightful; I always drink milkshakes, especially strawberry ones. When I went out with my friends to a milkshake house we had a competition who could drink the shake the fastest and obviously I won but my friend she took too much of a mouthful and squirted it all out on the waiter when he went by, it was HILARIOUS!

Strawberry milkshake comes from the United States but it was said years ago that it was made with whiskey and not milk.

How to make the strawberry milkshake

Ingredients you will need:

- Milk (cold)
- Whipped cream
- Strawberries (fresh)

Method:

1. First blend the strawberries and the milk
2. Then pour into a glass
3. Get out the whipped cream and squirt the biggest amount of cream on top.

Strawberry Milkshake

Strawberry milkshake,
you are a sweet treat for me,
strawberry milkshake,

Oh strawberry milkshake,
the way you taste,
with your presentation,
has a divine place in my house.

Trinity Perkins – Yr.7

<u>Honey</u>

Yummy honey, scrummy
In my tummy, better
Than chocolate, better
Than money, is my favourite
Honey.

A bee's fan, a Sheppard
Would prefer me better
Than a Lamb, I taste
Really nice on toast, but
Never try to post, I'm
Really, really runny
And really, really yummy

I am Honey

Riya Mody – Yr.6

Greek Shortbread Biscuits

Ingredients:

- 1 cup powdered sugar
- 1lb (2 cups) butter, softened
- 2 large egg yolks
- 1 teaspoon vanilla
- 4 cups flour
- 1 teaspoon baking powder
- 1 cup nuts, finely chopped
- Extra powdered sugar for coating
- 2 teaspoons vanilla essence

Instructions:

1. Preheat the oven to 180 degrees.
2. Beat the butter and sugar in a mixing bowl.
3. Add the egg yolk and beat.
4. Add vanilla essence and beat.
5. Add nuts, baking powder and flour.
6. Using your hands – press ingredients together to get a soft dough.
7. Shape 2 tablespoons of mixture at a time in to a moon shape. Repeat with the rest of the mixture.
8. Put the moon shapes on to a baking tray about 4cm apart.
9. Bake for 25 minutes.
10. Remove and let them cool down on a tray.
11. When cool – dust the moons with lots of icing sugar.

When we go to Cyprus my family make these all the time. We eat them after dinner and always get covered with icing sugar. These are my favourite desserts because they remind me of my holidays

Zoe Brooks - Yr.5

Chocolate Chip Cookies

1. Grease a baking tray using a little soft margarine and paper towel
2. Put margarine and sugar into a bowl and mix until light and fluffy
3. Put the flour and cocoa powder into a stove and sift into a bowl
4. Add the milk and chocolate chips and mix well together
5. Put 8-10 teaspoons of the mixture onto the greased tray, sprinkle on chocolate chips.
6. Bake for at least 20 minutes. Leave to cool for 3 minutes.
7. Then finally you can eat the chocolate chip cookies.

Hope you enjoy...

Sulily Jacques – Yr. 5

Chocolate Brownies

Ingredients:

- 90g of milk chocolate
- 150g of unsalted butter and extra for greasing
- 125g of plain flour
- 15g of cocoa powder
- ½ a teaspoon of baking power
- 1 pinch of salt
- 2 eggs
- 1tsp of vanilla extract
- 300g of soft light brown sugar

How to cook:

1. Preheat the oven to 180 degrees C, grease and line the base of the baking tin with a non-stick baking parchment.
2. Break the chocolate into a bowl and add the butter. Melt the butter and chocolate over a saucepan of barely simmering water, stirring occasionally.
3. Remove the bowl from the heat and allow the chocolate to cool slightly. Sieve the flour and cocoa powder, baking powder and salt into a separate bowl.
4. In a third bowl, beat the eggs and then add the sugar and vanilla extract. Stir the ingredients together until they are just combined.
5. Fold the melted chocolate into the beaten egg mixture. Then fold in the flour mixture. There should be no visible flour.
6. Spoon the mixture into the tin, smooth with a palette knife, and bake for 25 minutes. Allow it to cool in the tin before cutting into squares.

Sana Hamid – Yr.11

Chocolate milkshake

1) Melt the ice cream in the pan, stirring occasionally with a spatula.
2) Make the flavouring with the cocoa powder and milk.
3) When the ice cream has melted pour in the flavouring and stir vigorously.
4) Smash the ice with the meat hammer. You will add this later.
5) Pour the mixture into glass and add the ice!

My milkshake represents summer! As it is a cold and refreshing drink perfect for a hot summers day! It is easy to make, and is chilled by ice that will cool you down! The ice cream is creamy and stays cold even after melting! Leave in the fridge for half an hour to get a lovely refreshing drink!

Milkshake Poem

So rich so creamy,
The best you have ever tasted,
How can you resist it?
So rich and so creamy,
The best you have ever tasted,
The vanilla scent makes you senses dance.
So rich and so creamy,
The best you have ever tasted,
Chocolate sweet vanilla so sour.
So rich and so creamy,
The best you have ever tasted,
You can't wait to drink me again.
So rich and so creamy,
The best you have ever tasted.

Gemma Hook – Yr.7